POSTCARDS ON THE WAY TO HEAVEN

BRIAN MOUNTFORD

Postcards on the Way to Heaven

SPCK

First published in Great Britain 1997
Society for Promoting Christian Knowledge
Holy Trinity Church
Marylebone Road
London NW1 4DU

Copyright © Brian Mountford 1997

All rights reserved. No part of this book may be reproduced or transmitted in any form or by any means, electronic or mechanical, including photocopying, recording, or by any information storage and retrieval system, without permission in writing from the publisher.

Unless otherwise stated, biblical quotations are from the *Revised Standard Version* of the Bible © 1971 and 1952. Quotations from *The New English Bible* (NEB) © 1961, 1970 Oxford and Cambridge University Presses. Scriptures quoted from the *Good News Bible* published by The Bible Societies/HarperCollins Publishers Ltd UK © American Bible Society 1966, 1971, 1976, 1992.

British Library Cataloguing-in-Publication Data
A catalogue record of this book is available from the British Library

ISBN 0-281-05019-8

Typeset by David Gregson Associates, Beccles, Suffolk
Printed in Great Britain by Biddles Ltd, Guildford and King's Lynn

To the congregation of the University Church, Oxford,
the regulars, those at the edge and
those passing through.

Acknowledgements

The author and publishers would like to thank the following for permission to reproduce the material listed in which they own the copyright:

Faber & Faber for extracts from Philip Larkin, *Collected Poems* (1988) and from T. S. Eliot, *Collected Poems* (1963).

J. M. Dent for extracts from 'The Musician' by R. S. Thomas, *Collected Poems 1945–90*.

William Heinemann for extracts from Graham Green, *A Burnt-Out Case*.

Jonathan Cape for extracts from Bruce Chatwin, *The Song Lines*.

John Matthias and Ohio University Presses for extracts from 'Dedication to a Cycle of Poems on the Pilgrim Routes to Santiago de Compostela' by John Matthias in *Swimming at Midnight: Selected Shorter Poems*.

Contents

1	Don't forget to drop us a line	1
2	The Christian image repertoire	12
3	When the penny drops	37
4	The limits of imagery	47
5	God in music	54
6	Meeting God at the edge of faith	69
7	Walking with God	81
8	A pilgrimage to Prague	100
9	Heaven	113
	Notes	126

CHAPTER 1

DON'T FORGET TO DROP US A LINE

> The world is charged with the grandeur of God.
> It will flame out, like shining from shook foil ...
>
> Gerard Manley Hopkins, *God's Grandeur*

What excites me about Christianity is its surprise factor. Risky, challenging, revelatory, it bubbles with new ideas and pictures, uncovering God where you least expect, and questioning many of your spiritual, social, and political assumptions. It moves, it creates, and it changes lives. So I want to explore the *possibilities* of Christian faith, rather than attempt to summarize what I think Christians *ought to believe*. Don't get me wrong, I am not against tradition, on the contrary, I am very much for it, and couldn't be a Christian without it, but, as I hope to show (amongst other things) in the course of this book, tradition itself is fluid and on the move, and you can be true to your historical roots, while being open to the diversity of human experience. To put it another way, I want to create a theological environment which is broad enough and fertile enough for people who are not naturally religious types to find God in. So my emphasis has been more on exploration than settling down. Not that searching is the prerogative of non-religious types. In fact, most of my ideas have been worked out in dialogue with the faithful people of the congregations I have had the privilege to serve – and I am grateful to them for that.

However, if, as Gerard Manley Hopkins says, it is the *world* that is charged with the grandeur of God, then we probably need to step outside the confines of institutional Christianity to behold him. This seems to me particularly true in the rapidly changing society of the late twentieth century, where many of the old certainties are breaking down. The popular Christian response to this pluralism (or whatever you like to call it) has been an instinctive and defensive withdrawal behind the barricades of conservative faith. The attitude is safety first: history ended yesterday, so let's preserve what we've got at all costs, and let's not take the risk of further exploration.

Actually, Jesus warns of the foolishness of such a policy in the parable of the Talents; the master upbraids the cautious servant who has buried his talent to preserve it, and gives it to the servant who has risked his five talents on speculative investments, and made five talents more. To those that have shall more be given, and those who have not even what they have shall be taken away, says Jesus sternly (Matthew 25.14–30).

I believe that there are many people asking questions, both within the mainstream of Christianity and at its edge, who need to be set free to take the risks of exploration, and to travel wherever that road leads them, even when it goes to unexpected places.

What I have written arises out of my own attempt at that journey. You could describe it as notes on a spiritual journey, because as a working parish priest I have to write in the short spaces that become available between worship, meetings, visits, interviews, and administrative duties, and consequently the work has more in common with a diary than a highly organized, systematic thesis, which is not necessarily a bad thing. Perhaps it is more accessible than a *summa theologica*; we think and communicate in shorter gobbets these days – it is a feature of the mass media world – short, unconnected, bits.

That is why I thought I might call it *Postcards on the Way to Heaven*, because here are some communications from me to you that try to give the flavour of what I find exciting and compelling about the spiritual journey. But beware of taking my metaphor too literally. I am not simply saying, 'Wish you were here'. Postcards have writing on one side and *pictures* on the other...

One of the things that has interested me greatly is the importance of story-telling for theology. A story manages to suggest nuances and subtleties of meaning that are often absent from abstract statements, and a story can be very effective at turning a question back on the reader, or hearer, in such a way that we are helped to think for ourselves, and helped to make an insight part of our experience rather than leaving it as something theoretical and 'out there'. It is not by chance that the gospels are stories, or that Jesus taught in parables, or that large parts of the creeds are narrative in style.

In preaching, for example, it is widely recognized that illustrations are important; the congregation wakes up to a story, and nods off during long conceptual discourses. This was once demonstrated to me at a lecture where the speaker began by describing an accident he had seen on his way to the hall, in which a cyclist had been knocked from his bicycle by a hit-and-run motorist. The lecturer then admitted that he had made it all up – he hadn't seen an accident at all – but weren't we all on the edge of our seats as he told the story?

I have written a number of extended illustrations or short stories which are incorporated into the text of this book. These are the pictures on one side of the postcard. In one sense, if you write a story, you hope that it will speak for itself and not need interpretation. Indeed, if it doesn't speak for itself, it is not a very good story. However, when we send postcards we usually make connections between the picture and the message – this is the mountain where I fell down and broke my leg; in a sunset such as this I proposed to Penelope. I have tried to make connections in my theological postcards between the word-pictures and the writing on the other side, so that religious experience might possibly come alive in a new way.

Oh, you might say, but postcards are so trivial! Not always. An uncle of mine, who was an artist, used to write in a minuscule italic hand, with an extra-fine fibre tipped pen. When his postcards arrived, the children would say, 'Here's another dissertation from Douglas', and get out the magnifying glass to read about his latest adventures to ordinary places, which were always wittily and elegantly described.

Can you imagine it?

You might have said that Uncle Douglas was able to write these literary postcards, which made an ordinary place like the King George's Reservoir at Chingford seem as interesting as Lake Windermere, because he had a vivid imagination, and this is where we start. He saw potential. He saw things that the rest of us had missed: the bird life; he speculated about the lives of those who sailed their boats there; noticed the sheep grazing on the embankments, seemingly unfrightened by the constant 'growl' of the North London traffic.

Much has been written about the imagination in psychology and literature, and I leave that to the professionals. I find it helpful to think of the imagination as a personal image factory. I see the imagination as that function of the mind capable of translating ideas and experience into images, metaphors and symbols. It is a function that works two ways: first, by interpreting images created by other people, so that when you read a book or look at a picture, you have to use your imagination; and secondly by generating its own images, most obviously when a person thinks, speaks, writes, or draws.

In Christian theology it is very important not to confuse imagination with what is *imaginary*, in the sense of unreal or fanciful. An example of such use would be a child saying, 'I thought I heard a knock at the door', and her mother replying,

'No dear, it was only the wind. You must have *imagined* it.' The obvious theological fear is that when the imagination is linked closely with God talk, people might conclude that God is not real, but imaginary – as in a fairy tale. The idea that God talk doesn't refer to reality is something I would refute absolutely.

So it's a small irony that, in my sense, imagination is probably the *key* theological tool, because it sees the potential, the hidden possibilities, of both persons and things; discerning more and more of the infinite scope of God's creation. For instance, the supreme example of theological imagination is to think what it would be like to be in someone else's shoes, to try to get inside someone else's suffering or needs in such a way that you feel those needs so acutely you are compelled to act. That surely is the true meaning of 'You shall love your neighbour as yourself' – empathy, attention, *imagination*.

Thinking along the same lines, the incarnation could be seen as God's imagining what it would be like to be human, getting into our shoes. I can hear a chorus of protest: God didn't just *imagine* it, he *did it*. Of course that is right, but maybe I haven't got my point across. The image factory can explore ideas, even if we don't eventually settle on them as the answers to our questions. Imagination is to do with creativity, and if God is the creator of all that is, then God must have infinite imagination, and part of that imaginative creativity is that he chose to empty himself of his 'godness' to take the form of a servant, and to be born a human being, to step into our shoes (Philippians 2.6-8).

In view of all this, Christian theology, whether done by academics or by people on their way to work, must be interested in generating as diverse and rich a picture of God as possible, because God is infinite, and the more you see the more you understand. Yet even the analogy of a single picture, however broad its scope, isn't enough. It would be better perhaps to think of an artist's entire output. Cézanne, for instance, painted the same scene many times, and each time he saw something different - different shapes, light, colour, and so on. Theology also needs to paint the same scene over and over again, and to see the same scene painted by different artists. This has of course already happened. Not only has the *Adoration of the Magi*, for instance, been painted by Angelico, Dürer, Leonardo da Vinci, and Veronese, to name but a few, but the story of the Feeding of the Five Thousand is told in each of the four gospels, and there are numerous theories about how salvation works. So the Christian image factory has been hard at work across the centuries, producing ideas and models, books and pictures, music and poetry, some of which is sublimely beautiful like Mozart's *Requiem*, and some of which is vulgar and tasteless, like half the trinkets on sale at your average tourist shrine – Virgins with halos that flash like a Times Square illumination, or tacky verses in plastic frames.

Yet behind all this proliferation of imagery, I often think, is the deluding mirage that there must be a simple truth about God which, if grasped, would remove all need of imagery. This is the 'Holy Grail' mentality, the ultimate reductionism. The Grail, you remember, was thought to be the cup used by Christ at the Last Supper, and became the object of the quest of the Arthurian knights. Whoever looked into the cup would see the essence of God which no human language could describe. It's an appealing idea to be able to look, as it were, into the heart of God, but it is idolatry. Despite the imagery of the eucharist, where Christ is made present in bread and wine, God cannot be reduced to some juice in the bottom of a cup. Quite the opposite, it seems to me. Just as we use the model of the expanding universe for our understanding of the cosmos, so it might be helpful to realize that, if God is universal, our theological understanding can only ever be expanding and diversifying, and never reductive.

Let me try to explain what I am driving at with some more pictures of how I think the imagination works – some 'postcards' if you like. At the theatre the audience knows that the characters are only actors: Macbeth or Banquo's Ghost, say, are only actors, and that what they do, in one superficial sense, is not real. Yet, as the imagination is engaged by their acting, the play becomes real. So much so that occasionally a member of the audience will forget the convention and gasp at some injustice that is done. As a rule, we do not rush on to the stage to intervene in a fight or a murder because we know that the dagger has a retracting blade and that the blood is tomato ketchup. Yet, far from this being absurd, the imagination arouses real emotions – it has translated this portrayal of ambition, sin, and guilt (the theme of *Macbeth*), into real experience. Even the fantastic witches – the 'secret, black and midnight hags' – instead of seeming trivial, symbolize with spine-chilling effect an ambience of doom, and darkness, and evil.

So there is the question of what is real. Is reality to do necessarily with physical tangibility, or with significant meaning? Besides, is the transcendent God *physically* tangible? Jesus of Nazareth, God made man, certainly was physically tangible, but is the Christ of faith physically tangible? And, if not, are God and Christ real? To the Christian that is an absurd question; of course they are real. It takes us back to the old chestnut about the physical resurrection of Christ. Those who get very agitated about this should go back to the New Testament, to the gospel accounts, to the references in the Acts of the Apostles, and to Paul's 1 Corinthians 15. The answer is one of expanding ambiguity: the risen Christ appeared through closed doors, he was not immediately recognizable to Mary in the garden or to the disciples on the Road to Emmaus, he ate fish, he showed his wounds to Thomas, he appeared within a very short space of time in Jerusalem and Galilee, and St Paul claims of the resurrected body that 'it is sown a physical body, and raised a spiritual body'(1 Corinthians 15.44). The stories expand rather than simplify, and the message is that the ultimate reality is not so much about placing one's hands in the physical wounds of Christ, as about encountering the significant meaning of God, which will also be to experience the *love* of God.

But, back to another 'postcard' of the imagination at work. There is a significant difference between watching *Middlemarch*, or *Pride and Prejudice*, or *Sense and Sensibility* on screen and reading the novels for yourself. On screen the text is reduced to the barest narrative essentials, and even then important parts of the book have to be left out because of the constraints of time; the characters are personified by particular actors, whose two-dimensional photographs then appear on the video and book covers; and the location is defined by the director's choice. On the other hand, the reader of the novel must use her imagination to create the characters, the tensions, and the physical setting. Many would argue therefore that the reader has a fuller and more memorable experience than the viewer, because the imagination has to work harder.

Not that I wish to knock TV as some of the more supercilious dons do, disdainfully telling you that they have never even owned a set. TV may make couch potatoes of us all, but it also is the medium of our time, and in its way a stimulus to the imagination.

There was a brilliant series, entitled *Bard on the Box*, in which a producer had persuaded people from the Ladywood Estate in Birmingham to act some scenes from Shakespeare. They had little experience of acting and even less knowledge of Shakespeare, so they were frightened of making fools of themselves, and therefore they mocked serious drama and their own intellectual abilities in sentences littered with the 'f' word. The producer, Michael Bogdanov, commenting on their initial cynicism and negative attitude quoted Caliban from *The Tempest*:

You taught me language; and my profit on't
Is, I know how to curse . . .

With much nudging and giggling and egging on people came forward to learn lines and act scenes, and acted them excitedly with natural, unaffected vigour. Soon (and irrepressibly) imagery, words, and role play caught the imagination. Shakespeare was the ubiquitous talk of the estate, in bars, mother and toddler groups, and in a very rude drag show on a 'ladies only' night, when a drag queen performed the naming of bodily parts by the French princess from *Henry V* – with variations! The combined result of all these experiments was transforming for the individuals involved – expanding, purposeful, enlightening, affirming, and redeeming. Many found self-respect as they overcame their inhibitions and enjoyed doing something serious, which they had thought they weren't capable of doing. What had begun with cursing ended with pride in speech.

This transformation is the saving work of imagery and, from one point of view at least, a case of God's hiddenness being explored through art. It was a kind of resurrection achieved through the discovery of significant meaning and self-respect: I can do it, I can act, people want to watch me and are interested, and are responding, and when I have finished they shout for more.

Symbols and Devils

Symbols are closely connected with the imagination. A symbol is something which represents another reality, so that language and paintings are both symbolic in that sense, and at their best make those other realities more accessible, easier to relate to, and, if one can say so, more real.

In theology such language brings us into the realm of sacraments, which are often defined as 'outward and visible signs of inward and spiritual grace'. Thus water is the symbol of baptism, the joining of hands the symbol of marriage, and anointing with oil the symbol of healing. Somehow the symbols both represent and embody the relational nature of God who washes away sin and allows new relationship, who sanctifies the love of bride and bridegroom, and desires wholeness for those who are broken.

And curiously this is the etymology of the word 'symbol', which comes from the Greek *sum-ballein*, literally 'to throw with', or to throw together: thus 'to confer', and 'to meet with'. So a symbol is the coming together of one idea upon another, where the one illuminates the other; and a person who 'gets it together' is one who is integrated, which is precisely what happened to the people of the Ladywood Estate: they became more integrated human beings through the experience of creative imagination and drama.

If you were to ask yourself what is the etymological opposite of symbol, you would come up with *dia-ballō* - to 'throw apart', to 'scatter', and hence a 'slanderer' or 'false accuser', one who throws a spanner in the works, who drives a wedge between people, who breaks down relationship, who disintegrates. Thus diabolical, meaning devilish. In the gospel story of Jesus' Temptation in the Wilderness, and in the parable of the Sower, and at the Last Supper when the devil puts it in the mind of Judas to betray Jesus, the Greek word for devil is *diabolos*.

It is tempting to cite all the occasions in the gospels where Jesus heals those who are possessed by demonic power. Some are thrown about by the devils, into the fire, and on to the stone floor. Jesus casts out the *diaboloi*, and in doing so heals, draws together, composes, integrates. However, the word here is not *diaboloi*, but 'demons' and 'unclean spirits'. But the meaning still stands.

Post Script

Unpacking is a jargon word popular in some dialects of theologyspeak. 'Thank you, Professor, can you just *unpack* that for us?' means to explicate, explain, analyse, break down into component parts, translate, deconstruct. It's a word I never use except when returning from holiday. But it amuses me, and maybe throws light on the image of the image factory. The metaphor is of unpacking a suitcase and revealing the contents one by one; of lifting up the compressed articles and shaking out the creases.

Obviously the questioner has not packed the suitcase herself or she would already know what was in it; someone else has packed it, probably a theologian, maybe the professor. What the audience longs for is revelation and characterization. They could learn so much about the subject from the slow exposition of his/her clothes – when did he/she imagine wearing this? What is wrapped in this silk handkerchief? Why the camouflage jacket?

The more diverse the garments, the more we learn about the person who put them there; the more enigmatic, the more fascinated we become. This is a model for the potential of Christian imagery, like a suitcase full of tantalisingly diverse clues. Thus when a theological idea is *unpacked* we hope it will turn out to be as revealing and amazing as the magician's briefcase.

CHAPTER 2

THE CHRISTIAN IMAGE REPERTOIRE

> In a higher world it is otherwise, but here below to live is to change, and to be perfect is to have changed often.[1]
>
> J. H. Newman

Bags have to be packed for a journey, then unpacked, and repacked again at each stopping place in the unremitting discipline of managing clothes and equipment. In a sense this is what Christians do with their tradition; they enter a dialogue between tradition and experience, between tradition and changing culture, in which the tradition is repeatedly packed, unpacked, and repacked. Occasionally part of the kit becomes redundant and has to be jettisoned; sometimes a seemingly superfluous article comes in surprisingly handy.

The next part of the narrative is about unpacking texts, and finding that once they are out of the suitcase, they have an annoying habit of being too big to squeeze back in again.

In religion it is not always an easy jump from rational explanation to mystery, or vice versa. Perhaps some people are philosophers by nature, and others poets. Of course you can be both, but one of the problems for Western Christianity is the inbuilt tension between the two. Take a miracle like the story of Jesus turning water into wine – is this a scientific description of what happened, or a poetic account of the intoxicating power of Jesus' message? Both interpretations are valid, and complementary, and not the only ones available. Which just goes to illustrate the extremely creative *wordiness* of Christianity.

THE CHRISTIAN IMAGE REPERTOIRE

Christianity is a 'religion of the Book', the Bible, and therefore a religion of the word. It depends for its authority on Scripture, the Word of God, and prior to that on God himself who is the *Word*. At the creation God *spake* and it was done; in the stable at Bethlehem the infant Christ is the Word, the divine *Logos*, made flesh; and, later in John's Gospel, those who wish to be a part of Christ (branches on his vine) must obey his *words*, by keeping his commandments.

The nature of the biblical text has been widely debated, and the arguments are well known. The underlying belief amongst Christians is that the Bible is the divinely inspired word of God – a view which ranges in interpretation from belief that God guided the minds of the writers, to the belief that the writers were simply recording in their own words their experience of God's historical revelation. So, when we say that the text is divinely inspired, it does not necessarily mean that it has to be taken as an infallible *ex cathedra* statement by God, containing no symbols and no myths, just a pure line of unambiguous, definitive, unquestionable communication from God. It can also be seen as a collection of complex texts, characterized by editorial interpretation, human vision and human error, which despite (or because of) its versatility and variety, carries a message of good news and hope for humankind.

This second view is the one I take myself. The ambiguity and fluidity of the *storiness* of the Bible means that the reader has to be in a creative relationship with the text; the text is not a museum piece, but is 'in use', in the sense that the foundational narratives of Christianity constantly are being re-told and reread in worship, and in private, by people seeking to explore their relationship with God. It is the converse of the desire for reasons and explanations, because this exploration of God is a kind of impressionism, like Monet or Manet, in which the interaction of text and reader generates fresh images. Tradition, of which the biblical text is a part, is in principle passed on and handed down from one generation to another, particularly in the form of stories. In the process the tradition is constantly readapted to address the priorities of succeeding generations. And here it should be remembered that, historically, the biblical tradition has been assimilated, often by illiterate people, second-hand through art, re-telling, mystery plays, and so on. In other words, the method of passing on the tradition is not nearly as literal as we often imagine. The same is true this century with films such as *Exodus* and *Jesus of Nazareth*, musicals like *Joseph and the Technicolour Dreamcoat*, *Godspell*, and *Jesus Christ Superstar*, and in the continuing popularity of oratorios such as Handel's *Messiah* and Stainer's *The Crucifixion*.

In this discussion of imagery, verbal images are not to be confused with the graven images forbidden by the second commandment. The graven image is an inanimate object, superstitiously worshipped by those who are lazy enough (or frightened enough) to reduce God to a statue or fertility symbol. The graven image is a reduction of God, whereas the verbal image is an expansion of God. Someone (I don't know who) described Christian theology as 'the expansion of the image repertoire'. You start with a slimline statement, such as I believe in God, and then you have to amplify it with the stories and interpretations of both Scripture and experience. So, the verbal image is a building block of Christian storytelling and poetry, a part of God himself, who expressed himself as the Word made flesh, and the babble of language, universally understood at Pentecost, when the Holy Spirit descended upon the apostles. It is a kind of word play.

In fact the gospels could be described as 'word plays'; not just as in drama, but as in games, where ideas and images dart and dive, feinting to go this way and that in an infinity of possible moves. There are ironies and paradoxes within the mighty proclamations, such as Jesus' call to 'follow me' being qualified by the saying that you must lose your life to save it; or the paradox that the Word-made-flesh, as a baby in Bethlehem, cannot actually speak a word. T. S. Eliot in *Ash*

THE CHRISTIAN IMAGE REPERTOIRE

Wednesday speaks of 'the unstilled world' which 'whirled/ About the centre of the silent Word', and Lancelot Andrewes in his Christmas Day sermon of 1618, having made the same point says that, nevertheless, Christ 'speaks, and out of his crib...this day speaks to us'. I owe this quotation to the literary critic Valentine Cunningham, who suggests that this places the Word, or Christ, 'at the centre of a sign system of astonishing versatility'.[2] He means, I think, that Godliness and Christliness is there, potentially, in all language. That is a view I share and is what this particular chapter sets out to explore.

There is another bit of textual unravelling which Valentine Cunningham uses to illustrate his argument. In 1 Peter 2.21 Christ is described as the example in whose footsteps Christians ought to follow. The Greek for *example* (a one-off word in the New Testament, a *hapaxlegomenon*) is *hupogrammos*. A *hupogrammos* is the line of writing written out by a teacher for pupils to copy in order to learn their letters. It usually contains all the letters of the alphabet, as does 'the quick brown fox jumps over the lazy dog' in English. While it might seem an odd, or even diminishing, image to think of Christ as a line of writing in a child's exercise book, we have to remember that Christ is also described (in the Book of Revelation) as the Alpha and the Omega, the beginning and the end – i.e. he contains all the letters of the alphabet, the complete A–Z. Thus, in the metaphor of the *hupogrammos*, Christ contains all language potential – which is what you might expect of the eternal Word of God. And that it should be so lowly an image as a child's exercise, associated in modern times with the imposition of 'fifty lines' for bad behaviour, is not surprising for one who said that unless you become as little children you shall in no way enter the kingdom of heaven.

This is an example of how Scripture proliferates and intensifies meaning, instead of narrowing it down to an unequivocal definition. Biblical texts pose at least as many questions as they answer, which is a strength rather than a weakness;

not a sign of uncertainty or lack of conviction, but evidence of the power and creativity of the text. Of course some texts are rather more memorable than others. In the New Testament the Christmas and Easter stories spring to mind, along with the Prodigal Son, the Good Samaritan, and Paul's first letter to the Corinthians – 'Though I speak with the tongues of men and of angels and have not love ...' (1 Corinthians 13.1). These are texts people keep returning to, presumably because they are an endless source of light for the spiritual journey.

I think the point is underlined when Christ himself does some textual exegesis.

> You have heard it said of old time an eye for an eye and a tooth for a tooth, but I say unto you ... if anyone strikes you on the right cheek, turn to him the other also.' (Matthew 5.38–9)

He is no literalist, but draws out a subtext of meaning, which gets to the heart of the matter. It comes as a great surprise to those who thought that ancient Scripture was somehow 'given' or unchangeable, to discover that Jesus doesn't see it that way. For him the ancient verse opens a major moral question – the proper response to aggression – which he treats in a new and radical way by proposing that people should 'turn the other cheek'. This has provoked ethical debate among individuals, politicians, soldiers, and lawyers across the Christian centuries.

This commentary by Jesus on the traditional Jewish law is an interesting example of how, even within the so-called 'sacred' text of the Bible, tradition is on the move and not something static and given. It may be that tradition is sometimes appealed to as unquestionably authoritive when someone wants it to back up their argument, but that is a mirage.

Of course it is true that from time to time traditions have been set down on papyrus or formulated into creedal statements, giving them an air of permanence. But these texts only

THE CHRISTIAN IMAGE REPERTOIRE

give a snapshot of where tradition happened to be in AD 65 when Mark wrote his Gospel, or in AD 325 or AD 381 when the 'Nicene' creeds were formulated. Even in these cases we do not possess the original documents, and there is always argument about how much the traditions have been tweaked and changed between the time of the original manuscript and the discovery of the earliest surviving version. My point is that, quite apart from the diversifying nature of imagery and metaphor, the foundational texts themselves were growing and diversifying while they were being formed.

However, it is the leaven of imagery rising in the textual lump that fascinates me most. Discussing what makes a 'classic' text, George Steiner argues that 'the generation of obstacles may be one of the elements which keep a 'classic' vital'.[3] If applied to the sacred text, this might seem a scurrilous view to some Christians. Obstacles cause people to stumble, and Jesus said that those who cause searchers to stumble should have a millstone tied round their neck and be dropped into the sea. But obstacles also cause people to stop and think. Valentine Cunningham is saying something similar when he describes classic texts as 'fathering' texts – pieces of writing, or scripture, which demand to be reread because they go on requesting light from the reader. So these memorable texts tease, and prod, and cajole the reader into doing more work for herself – which is creative and good. You don't just look up the answer in the New Testament, you are set a-thinking.

Speaking of fathering texts, I am reminded of Gerard Manley Hopkins' poem, *Pied Beauty*, in which he praises God for fathering-forth 'All things counter, original, spare, strange'. By 'counter' I think he means something like 'opposite', 'different'. The line paints a picture of what is creative, risky, unconventional, new – the sort of things that so annoyed the Pharisees of the gospels. Could this be what is meant by Scripture being 'divinely inspired' – God in the text, fathering-forth images?

The prologue to St John's Gospel is a fine example of such a classic text: it doesn't explain or define the nature of God's incarnation so that you can say, OK, message received and understood. It asks to be reread; and it *is* reread all over the world in carol services every Christmas, when it rekindles a wonderment at the mystery of the incarnation, making people think again about the nature of their own spiritual experience.

Moreover, the prodigality of these texts is enough for everyone. What is fathered is as diverse as the people who read or hear them. Christianity tends to encourage a myth about itself that it is uniform and orthodox, as if you could buy a standard model, like buying a lampshade in East Berlin before the Wall came down, when they were all identical. If you owned a lampshade, anyone would be surprised if it were different from theirs. Not so with Christianity, although some people think it ought to be like that for the sake of security, and purity, and knowing where you stand. But the fathering texts of the Bible do not spawn clones. Like God, who spake to create, they give birth to a multitude of unique spiritual lives, each with a different face, each made in the image and likeness of God.

In practice the biblical texts are used in a very flexible way, even by those who regard themselves as purists. As I say, there are no autograph manuscripts available to see what the authors actually wrote; people are far more likely to be purist about particular versions – committed to 'old' language or politically correct language. And rather than having a clear picture of St Luke's view of Jesus, or St John's view, they are more likely to remember edited highlights from the New Testament and call it 'the Gospel'. In the end the purity of the text doesn't matter. Valentine Cunningham makes this point in relation to John Bunyan, who had the highest regard for the divine inspiration of Scripture, yet felt at liberty to stretch and manipulate it in his *Pilgrim's Progress*, and other writings. He saw no problem about improvising on the biblical story so long as he brought people to Christ. Thus he allowed the text to bring forth its increase.

This way of thinking about textuality grows out of the literary critical method known as 'deconstruction'. Undoing the text might seem an over-rationalistic reductionism, but in Cunningham's hands it is leading to an expansion of images and insights so prolific as to be almost like speaking in tongues. His book, *In the Reading Gaol*, from which some of these arguments are taken, challenges the ordinary reader, and the theological reader, to learn a whole new and extravagant vocabulary.

So what do I conclude from this? I conclude that I believe in the biblicalness of Christianity. All Christians must be biblical Christians, Word Christians, People of the Book. No section of the Church can be more biblical than another, neither can any group justify a claim, as it were, to *own* the Bible as its exclusive resource. The literalists must get loose and take the lid off the great image repertoire, and the non-literalists must recognize that the great image repertoire is there boiling over as a resource they cannot possibly go without. Their spirituality must be shaped and fathered by the biblical narrative, allowing it to work and weave its spell – its Godspell – of imagery.

But is the only scripture helpful to Christian spiritual development *Holy* Scripture? Obviously not. Bunyan wrote his *Pilgrim's Progress* as a grand gloss on Holy Scripture in order to bring people to a deeper faith. The Church Fathers wrote commentaries on the great theological themes. Religious poets, such as Herbert, Milton, and Hopkins, developed spiritual themes in verse. But what about the literature that sets out with no confessional intent at all – *secular* literature? If Christ, the Word-made-flesh, is also the A–Z of language potential, then Christians should not be surprised to find revelation and spiritual enlightenment in writing that never set out to provide it. The theological reasoning behind this is that God is the God of the whole creation, and those writers whose vision and scope is universal will reflect on spiritual questions alongside the political, aesthetic, moral, and social ones.

For the sake of clarity let me set out my position: when it comes to Christian *theology*, I regard the biblical texts as first order texts, theological writing (including Augustine, Aquinas, religious poetry, sermons etc.) as second order texts, and writing in general as third order texts. But – and this is very important – I do not mean first, second, and third orders to indicate relative quality, but to identify different categories of theological writing. Put simply, my point is that Holy Scripture is uniquely important because it tells of the historic incarnation, but all writing holds something for theological enquiry. Professor David Brown makes a similar point when he argues that non-biblical tradition differs *in degree* but *not in kind* from biblical tradition, with God no less active within it.[4]

Sermon on the back of a Postcard

Preachers often write their sermon notes on a postcard. A card is easier to hold than A4 sheets, which tend to flap around, or droop over the lectern.

So long as I can remember I have thought that Christ cannot be imprisoned in churchy metaphors, and that the incarnation requires the widest frame of reference. As a theological student I wrote a sermon for a sermon class which took for its text a passage from the opening of D. H. Lawrence's novel, *The Rainbow*. I began to describe, in Lawrence's words, the earthborn life of the Brangwens on Marsh Farm on the northern border of Nottinghamshire. 'They knew the intercourse between heaven and earth,' I began,

> sunshine drawn into the breast and bowels ... They took the udder of the cows, the cows yielded milk and pulse against the hands of the men, the pulse of the blood of the teats of the cows beat into the pulse of

the hands of the men ... But the women looked out from the heated, blind intercourse of farm-life, to the spoken world beyond.

After I finished there was a long silence. I could see the Principal's face becoming volcanic. Then he exploded and said it was the most sensual sermon he had ever heard, and to me the word 'sensual' sounded like Vesuvius erupting. I began to shift apprehensively in my chair. I had only been trying to illustrate my understanding of the incarnation, but I was left in no doubt that this kind of sermon, if preached in a parish, would lose more souls than it would win.

It must have been a very gauche sermon (I no longer have a copy), but I was not trying to shock or be clever. I was simply trying to say that the *whole* of life is a proper subject for theological reflection, and that Lawrence's description of the farmer's relationship with the environment in deeply sensual and sexual language is not only honest and innocent, but enables us to see the creation in a way that perhaps we had not seen it before. Besides, Jesus himself frequently used farming metaphors to make a theological point: ploughing, sowing, harvesting, separating the wheat from the chaff – not quite the heated, blind intercourse of farm life, but certainly Christ located God in a number of places that the Pharisees considered out of bounds.

Twenty years after that sermon I wanted an altar-piece for the University Church in Oxford, and discovered that in the basement of the Ashmolean Museum there was a store of paintings never seen by the public. One of these, by a sixteenth century Italian, Francesco Bassano, depicted the angels appearing to the shepherds near Bethlehem. In the foreground there is a massive brown milch cow which dominates the picture. She is being milked by one of the shepherds, while the other shepherds and their sheep are relegated to the left and right sides of the picture. In the top left-hand corner, minute and bathed in light, stands Bethlehem.

POSTCARDS ON THE WAY TO HEAVEN

When the Diocesan Advisory Committee met to decide whether they could approve the hanging of the picture in St Mary's, one of them said what a pity it was I couldn't find a more 'religious' painting, by which, I suppose, he meant a crucifixion or a resurrection. But I remembered that 'the pulse of the blood of the teats of the cows beat into the pulse of the hands of the men', and all the incarnational vigour that I had felt on that particular day of sermon judgement. So I managed to win the Committee over by arguing that the Word becoming flesh was the centrepiece of Christian belief, on which all subsequent understandings of Christ depend. What, for example, would the crucifixion mean if it were not for this picture, this prior picture which qualified all subsequent theology? Here God enters the lives of simple people as they work at their ordinary tasks, and his presence arouses astonishment and hope.

But there was one another compelling image in my sermon text: the women of Marsh Farm knew the instinctive sensuality of farm life, yet it was not enough for them; they strained to reach out to the world of 'speaking' and 'utterance'. They wanted culture and thought, a sort of intellectual reflection and theology of the givenness of things. They wanted the flesh made word. This applied not only to farm life, but to religion as well.

Later in the novel Will and Anna Brangwen visit Lincoln Cathedral so that Will can show his wife the place that fills him with instinctive spiritual awe:

> ... he pushed open the door, and the great, pillared gloom was before him, in which his soul shuddered and rose from her nest ... Here in the church the 'before' and 'after' were folded together, all was contained in oneness.

For Will Brangwen the cathedral symbolizes the possibility of fulfilment in an unfulfilled, frustrated life. But for Anna, while the experience is impressive, the cathedral represents an imprisonment of her feelings. As she looks at the roof she would rather see the sky above; she does not want to be contained or limited by religion.

So their responses to the same religious symbol are in stark contrast to one another. Anna insists that a symbol cannot be all in all. It is to be an introductory experience, not a consummatory one, as it is for him.

Will is disillusioned by Anna's dissatisfaction. She is trapped and wants to be free. They had both had their eyes drawn to the altar, but while Anna was moved, it was for her nevertheless 'barren, its lights gone out. God burned no longer in the bush'.

Anna drew his attention to the imps and gargoyles which

> winked and leered, giving suggestion of the many things that had been left out of the great concept of the church. However much there is inside here, there's a good deal they haven't got in, the little faces mocked. He was forced to admit that there was life outside the church.

Subsequently, the story tells us, he would go to his little local church, and play the organ, and train the choir, and do practical jobs, preserving the fabric and attending to its upkeep. He settled for a humdrum life – 'If only there were not some limit to him, some darkness across his eyes! He had to give in at last to himself. He must submit to his own inadequacy, the limitation of his being.'

Here is the universal human anxiety about self-worth; the cry for personal identity and purpose within the cosmic, mind-bending scale of things. It is what might you might call the *incarnational ache*, the yearning for God, and the uncertainty of whether God is actually present. In the list of those things from which people believe they need to be saved, this is perhaps the greatest – the incarnational ache. The Word needs to be made flesh, but the flesh needs to be made word – articulated and given meaning.

Once again the expansion of the image repertoire leads to fresh theological insight – theology seen from a new angle – even when the symbol is the milking of a cow, in a novel, or behind the altar.

Larkin about with Religion

More recently I have explored the same theme of religious imagery in relation to other writers whose work I have admired. I gave a talk to students entitled 'Larkin about with Religion', and it was the first time I had filled an auditorium. Of course it was Larkin, not me, who was the draw. Some people came, I imagine, because they wanted to see how I would reconcile depressive, fatalistic old Larkin with Christian hope and assurance. Wasn't he a negative and embittered character, exposed in his letters, and Andrew Motion's biography, as immoral and corrupt? And, judging from what he says in *Vers de Société*, wasn't he a proselytizing anti-Christian?

> No one now
> Believes the hermit with his gown and dish
> Talking to God (who's gone too); the big wish
> Is to have people nice to you ...

And what about his life-denying cynicism? In the famous poem about parents:

> Man hands on misery to man.
> It deepens like a coastal shelf.
> Get out as quickly as you can,
> And don't have any kids yourself.

But poetry, of all literary forms, plays on the ambiguity and suggestiveness of language. Sometimes it is hard to believe that the poet can have intended all the subtle connections that critics find in their work. The title of the Larkin poem most often quoted by clergy, *Church Going*, is itself ambiguous; is this to be a poem about going to church, or about the institutional Church going ... down the spout?

Is Larkin actually peddling a doctrine of the irretrievable pointlessness of life when he says, 'and don't have any kids yourself'? Is that his last word on the matter, or is it a tongue-in-cheek challenge to the reader – go on, you don't really believe me, do you?

A very great deal of Christian language is poetic, and duplex in this way – not duplicitous in the sense of being double-dealing, but multi-layered and evocative, seeking a response, making people think for themselves as the parables of Jesus do. Christian language ought to ask questions, and the questions are the raw material of faith. Maybe it is the case that all who ask questions about meaning and relationship are in a sense asking *religious* questions.

When Larkin describes *Mr Bleaney* in the poem of that name, he depicts a sad man who lived in a bed-sit with

> upright chair, sixty watt bulb, no hook
> Behind the door, no room for books and bags.

Sparse, temporary accommodation, for a sparse, temporary life. It is a moving poem because the reader senses a desire to rescue some purpose and meaning for this particular life (partly Larkin's own, or so he would have you believe) trapped as it is in inescapable ordinariness. Theologically he is showing that in his experience of life there is actually *something to be saved from*. It is a poem about what I have just called the incarnational ache – the yearning for God, and the fear that God is not there – and he has, out of the depths of a finely observed despair, identified something human beings need to be saved from which many people are not ready to own up to – the pain of not being loved. Thus, I reckon, *Mr Bleaney* is a compassionate poem, on the grounds that its acute observation of loneliness and despair necessarily draws compassion from the reader, and strikingly illustrates what I mean by the raw material of religious enquiry.

Larkin's poetry generally questions the purpose of life – asks whether love and fulfilment are anything more than illusions – and reveals a prematurely haunting fear about his own death. What is engaging to so many people is that he does this from the point of view of the ordinary bloke in the pub, with his ordinary suburban, politically incorrect values. There's a lot of nudge, nudge, wink, wink, know what I mean. Arnold, in *Self's the Man*,

> married a woman to stop her getting away,
> now she's there all day.

In *Aubade* he begins,

> I work all day, and get half drunk at night,

but this is a poem about lying awake at night thinking about death –

> Unresting death, a whole day nearer now.

He calls this experience

> a special way of being afraid
> No trick dispels. Religion used to try,
> That vast moth-eaten musical brocade
> Created to pretend we never die.

Don't some evangelists claim that those who protest loudest against religion are the most ripe for conversion? I sometimes feel this about Philip Larkin, and because so much of what he said was negative and pessimistic, those poems which express optimism are all the more precious, because hard won against the odds.

In *Church Going* he describes a visit to an empty country church. His initial approach is mocking; most people take their hats off when they enter a church, but he takes off his 'cycle-clips in awkward reverence'. At the lectern he reads some verses from the Bible, and says, ' "Here endeth", much more loudly than I'd meant'. As he leaves he donates an Irish sixpence, and reflects the place was not worth stopping for.

'Yet stop I did', he says, and after musing whether churches are museums, places of superstition, or just good for Christmas, births, marriages, and deaths, he admits that it pleases him to stand there in silence:

A serious house on serious earth it is

in which

... someone will forever be surprising
A hunger in himself to be more serious ...

So, while he creates an atmosphere of mocking scepticism about all church represents, he is surprised by a sense of hunger in himself to be more serious about it. This is the hunger of raw religious enquiry experienced by so many. Christianity takes this enquiry – what shall I do to inherit eternal life? – and offers the narrative of the gospels as a framework against which to shape spiritual ideas.

There is another poem, *The Explosion*, in which he shows the hunger-to-be-more-serious partly overlaid with Christian biblical imagery. It is the story of a mining disaster. A sense of foreboding is seen in the shadows that point towards the pithead as the men stomp down the lane to start their shift.

One of them finds a nest of lark's eggs and hides them in the grass to collect on his way back.

> At noon, there came a tremor; cows (cows again!)
> Stopped chewing for a second; sun,
> Scarfed in a heat-haze, dimmed.

Note the allusion to the crucifixion: 'From the sixth hour (noon) there was darkness over all the land until the ninth hour ... and the earth shook and the rocks were split' (Matthew 27.45, 51).

At the subsequent memorial service the preacher speaks of the comfort of God's house and the hope of eventually seeing one's loved ones 'face to face'. And for a second the

> Wives saw the men of the explosion
> Larger than in life ... walking
> Somehow from the sun towards them,
> One showing the eggs unbroken.

It is a kind of resurrection appearance, only spoiled by Larkin's inability to resist comparing the wives, who see this vision 'for a second', with the cows in the field which are startled by the explosion, 'for a second'. But the men, in the resurrection, are 'walking somehow from the sun'; and one thinks of the pun in English, immortalized by George Herbert, between the sun that rises and the Son of God, so that in a sense the men are bathed in the light of Christ. Then, finally, there is that very positive image of hope and new life – 'One showing the eggs unbroken'. It was a poignant moment in the third stanza when the miner hid the eggs, and it was plain he would never come back to collect them, and a poignant image in the women's vision that one man showed those very eggs, with all their promise of new life.

This is no attempt from the Christian point of view to claim Larkin as 'one of us'. I am sceptical of the propaganda ploy which lines up the famous – in sport, the media, or whatever – and tries to win converts by saying, if it's good enough for them, it's good enough for you. In any case, Larkin was probably whatever the opposite of a saint is.

So would I be happy for *The Explosion* to be read in church? Yes, I would. Would I be happy for *This be the Verse*, with its notorious 'f' word in the first line, to be read in church? No, I wouldn't – and I ask myself whether I am just being a prude. The theological answer has to do, I think, with the fact that since Christ is celebrated as the divine Word of God, there is something blasphemous about the use of abusive language in the very context where people hope that their vision of Christ will be most clarified. Besides this particular poem is essentially nihilistic, and in a significant way the reading of a text in worship implies approval. Therefore, whenever freedom of choice is given in worship, a judgement has to be made as to what will enhance spiritual insight and what will cloud it.

Those planning weddings and memorial services often ask for non-biblical readings these days. Instinctively I balk at their requests, which is very narrow-minded and hypocritical of me. I feel insulted on behalf of Christianity, and want to stand up for the Bible, because I was brought up to think that the only readings suitable for Christian worship are from Christianity's defining text, and here are these people implying that although this text might be good enough for you Christians, it's not quite good enough for us. Also I believe it right to resist those who want to minimize the Christian content of a church service – whether because of genuine uncertainty of belief, or the crude consumerist view that churches are public places available for any sort of rites-of-passage-type ritual. I think you have to keep the integrity of churches: they stand for Christian faith and Christian values. If people want to dignify secular celebrations let them use the grander secular public buildings – in Oxford, the Sheldonian Theatre would be a good choice, although that was built at the expense of an Archbishop of Canterbury!

Having said that, I am immediately aware of the dangers of exclusivism, and that I am risking losing the very breadth of image repertoire that I have been arguing for. But I don't want to compromise the integrity of Christian worship.

Two examples occur to me which show how difficult it is to know where to draw the line. The first was the memorial service for the poet John Wain, held in my church in 1995. Five of his own poems were read, along with *Pied Beauty* by Gerard Manley Hopkins, and *Afterwards* by Thomas Hardy. There was nothing from the Bible, and after the blessing the Crouch End All Stars played *On the Sunny Side of the Street* and *Ain't Misbehaving*. Yet it was a service of high spiritual significance and value.

The second is the extraordinary spin-off from the film *Four Weddings and a Funeral* which saw sales of W. H. Auden's poetry rocketing. His poem *Funeral Blues* had been read at the eponymous funeral by a homosexual friend of the deceased. 'He was my North, my South, my East and West/ My working week and my Sunday rest'. Faber and Faber immediately published a slim volume of ten Auden poems under the title *Tell me the Truth about Love*. I was given a copy by a bishop. It asked Christianity's most fundamental question, what is the truth about love? But it asked it in a genuinely agnostic way. The Christian would reply, if you want the truth about love, look at Christ. *Funeral Blues* has a final despairing line – 'Nothing now can ever come to any good'. Somehow this is countered by the expanding image of love, and Love. In an unexpected way a popular film and a publisher's commercial flair combine to generate a public theological discussion on the relation between God and Love.

The Bard and the Saint

Just occasionally it is possible to superimpose one text upon another and, instead of seeing a jumble of incomprehensible signs, there are areas of surprising readability. I did this with

THE CHRISTIAN IMAGE REPERTOIRE

Paul's passage about the whole armour of God in Ephesians, and bits of Shakespeare's *Macbeth*, so you might say these are postcards from Stratford-upon-Avon and Ephesus. The similarities clicked in my mind when I was trying to illustrate how a literalist biblical interpreter must have to accept at least some scriptural passages as metaphorical. For example 'the whole armour of God' is clearly not actual armour but righteousness, peace and faith. That much is straightforward and easy. However, the nature of the enemy being resisted with the armour of God and the sword of the Spirit is not so clear. 'We are not contending against flesh and blood,' says St Paul, 'but against the principalities, against the powers, against the world rulers of this present darkness, against the spiritual hosts of wickedness in the heavenly places' (Ephesians 6.12). What kind of language is this? Is the twentieth-century reader to imagine supernatural evil powers, with balaclavas pulled down over their faces, yomping round the universe committing acts of terrorism against all that is good and true? Some people do believe in the physical reality of evil forces, but most accept the verdict of physics and psychology that this is unlikely. So does that make Paul's writing irrelevant to the present day?

Now let me superimpose on the Ephesians text a speech of Lennox on the morning after Duncan's murder in *Macbeth*.

> The night has been unruly: where we lay,
> Our chimneys were blown down; and, as they say,
> Lamentings heard in the air; strange screams of death,
> And prophesying with accents terrible
> Of dire combustion and confused events
> New hatch'd to the woeful time. The obscure bird
> Clamour'd the livelong night: some say the earth
> Was feverous and did shake. (Act 2.III)

Was that night really accompanied by supernatural events in the air? Or is this part of the poetic world of 'secret, black and midnight hags', created by Shakespeare as an ominous context for murder most foul? Imagery of blackness and darkness pervades the play, and is even used with ironic self-knowing by the murderers themselves, as for example Lady Macbeth's 'Come, thick night/And pall thee in the dunnest smoke of hell', or Macbeth's 'Macbeth hath murdered sleep'. This is a play of the night.

As the two texts come into focus there seems a surprising coincidence between St Paul's 'world rulers of this present darkness', and Shakespeare's 'unruly night' with 'lamentings heard in the air'. Whether St Paul or Shakespeare actually believed in the reality of supernatural powers of evil doesn't really matter. What we recognize is that evil has ramifications which can seem to reverberate in the air. It is an entirely contemporary image too, in the sense of speaking of 'bad vibes' between people who dislike each other, or of an 'atmosphere' in a family where relationships are bad. Evil is hard to contain, as any temporarily undiscovered criminal knows; it seems to leak out into the air. Macbeth wanted power and kingship and made the mistake of thinking that a simple assassination could provide it; but, quite apart from the logistical difficulties of executing the perfect crime, he hadn't taken into account the psychological effect: the guilt, the self-detestation, the fear, the disintegration of his mind. His tragedy is the tragedy of unredeemed humanity writ large.

St Paul recognizes the same human potential for tragedy, and describes it as the threat from the 'principalities and powers', and 'spiritual hosts of wickedness'. The way to overcome them, he suggests, is to put on godliness as a protection – righteousness, peace and faith. And it is a compelling image which feeds in to the picture of a cosmic battle between good and evil.

From a Far Country

If the Christian spiritual and theological vocabulary can be expanded by drawing on secular texts which do not set out to be theological, then the biblical texts are also capable of reaching out of their sacred environment to embrace the secular. This must be their main purpose, that they are not confined to the cloister, but incarnated in the world. The parables function exactly in this way. Their story-lines are drawn from secular experience – farming, politics, tricky relationships – and spiritual meaning attaches to those themes as they are told.

Take the case of the Prodigal Son (Luke 15); it does not and cannot have an absolute teaching or 'right' meaning. It is an ambiguous and fluid story that gives rise to a multiplicity of readings, and that is why people like to hear it re-told, because each time it draws out new ideas and insights. A fathering text in more ways than one!

Let me attempt a paraphrase to illustrate what I mean by the fluidity of the text.

Greedy and adventurous, the younger son exploits his father's generosity and then betrays his father's trust. He is like the modern drug-taker, joy-rider, or your worst fears about your own children. But is it his fault? Why do children leave home? Has the boy been driven out by his parents' possessiveness and over-exacting discipline?

'Hang on,' interrupts a literalist heckler, 'that's not in the text. The father is God, so how can you say the boy's behaviour is his parents' fault? You've been reading too much Freud.' I reply by asking where it says that the father is God, or that the boy did not have a mother. Is it improper to try to understand the boy's motivation?

Anyway he takes his money and runs. When the cash runs out he is desperate, an exile abroad, unable to speak the language, living amongst swine, which according to his religion are ritually unclean. He seems to have deserved all he gets, and yet his story arouses compassion, because, in a sense, he is a type for all who reach the limits of isolation and despair, whether they deserve to or not. His experience is not so different from a person in a refugee camp, or a member of an ethnic minority tormented for being culturally different, or a lonely student in a strange town.

Eventually he says to himself, this is crazy, my dear old dad treats his servants a hundred times better than this. If I go back home he might take me in as one of them. He feels deeply penitent, and extremely sorry for himself. The two emotions merge into each other. But he also knows his dad won't be able to resist him.

Indeed, not. Dad runs to meet him, puts out the bunting, prepares a feast, puts a ring on his finger as a sign of restored authority in the household. It's all a bit like a wedding, and we remember that Jesus often depicts heaven as a wedding, as in his stories about the wise and foolish virgins, and the guest without a wedding garment.

'How dare you suggest that God is a soft touch?' shouts the heckler. 'He is just and righteous and requires repentance before he offers forgiveness. You mustn't water down the doctrine of forgiveness. He only restores the boy to his household because he has confessed that he has sinned against heaven and in his father's sight.'

I point out smugly that in the story the son was still 'far off' when his father ran to him 'and fell on his neck and kissed him', so he hadn't had time to make his confession.

I ask you, then, is this just a good story, or is it about you and God, about the refugee and the exile, or about life's failures and God?

'There you are,' laughs the literalist heckler, 'you admit that the father is God after all.'

'Yes, but not quite in the way you put it. You want to limit the story's application and resonances, as if to say there is a right and a wrong way of reading this scripture. I want to say that the point of the story, and others like it, is that there are no right answers, and that Jesus is saying, work it out for yourself.'

As I write this chapter the Western leaders are trying to

decide the appropriate role for the United Nations troops in the Balkans. News reports describe atrocities suffered at the hand of the Serbs in which families have been broken up, husbands separated from wives, and children from fathers. People have been taken into fields and shot. It is reminiscent of Auschwitz. How can this be redeemed? It was a question asked of the Nazi concentration camps, whether this was the truly unforgivable sin, and whether the excrescence of such evil in human history disproved the existence of God?

Maybe the Prodigal Son is a parable which can be read alongside these threatening theological questions as a kind of commentary, as a template of Christian understanding on which to measure a theology of Auschwitz and Bosnia. There is the reckless and penitent son. The readily forgiving father, and the cold older brother; civil war within the family reconciled by grace which is poured out like expensive ointment over the feet of Jesus.

But the story hasn't finished yet. What about the older brother – loyal, hard-working, dull, humourless, sanctimonious; jealous as hell of the wastrel kid brother who can do no wrong? Did he go out to find the lost brother? Oh no. Sibling rivalry is a powerful emotion. He was glad to see the back of him. It is a great twist to the story. But what is it about, what does it mean? Is it about you and God? Is it about religious people? Or hypocrites? About those who talk about God's love for sinners, but don't want that sort of person in the house, or perhaps are jealous of their adventurous spirit? Is it about the Western leaders who won't or can't stop the ethnic cleansing? Is it about Serbs? You see my point – this is an image-generating text.

Like the literalist critic, I also see in the parable a discussion of the nature of sin and forgiveness. But which is the greater sin – to have squandered your inheritance on riotous living, or to have stayed at home and taken no risks at all? There's an echo of the parable of the Talents again, where the one who buried his talent for safety's sake, had to hand it over to the one who had made ten talents. Grossly unfair? Go and risk all for the kingdom of God – including your interpretation of the Bible!

CHAPTER 3

WHEN THE PENNY DROPS

> What a miracle claims about the universe is that on some occasion the universe 'comes alive' in a personal sort of way.
>
> Ian Ramsey

The unpacking of the image repertoire suitcase is nothing less than miraculous. Experiences are translated into signs and signs become miracles – it's not such a big step – and a postcard from East Germany might begin to explain why.

Red-nosed Theology

I have an acrobatic toy clown that spins on an axis along parallel bars. The axis is a short metal rod held in his hands, with the weight of his legs and torso equally distributed above and below. He was made in the German Democratic Republic in the 1970s. It's not high art, but I think it's creative and imaginative. It demonstrates the force of momentum: you set the clown spinning with a flick of the finger and he continues to somersault to the other end of the bars. I still find this profoundly fascinating – that what I set in motion can continue so energetically beyond my initial action. It is a wonder to me, as it is a wonder to many young children, even though I sort of understand the physics. But he is also a clown, created in a repressive society which was unfunny and needed laughter. The materials are cheap, and the construction is simple. Its simplicity is part of its beauty, and its understated decoration part of its appeal.

White-faced with a red pointy hat, my clown questions

what it means to be 'creative'. He is like Uncle Douglas' postcards, seeing the ordinary in new ways. What could be more prosaic than the repetitive dullness of life for a communist worker in a toy factory? Yet that worker has used the limited materials available, to give pleasure to a child, demonstrate the wonder of motion, and convey laughter and lightness in a grim and heavy society. That in my book is three miracles already.

We sometimes speak of 'creative tension', or how suffering can be the catalyst for creativity – the artist in a freezing attic, the musical composition forged out of depression, the pain of childbirth. Well, my clown symbolizes the durability of hope under repression. I also have a strong feeling that he was *lovingly* made, by which I mean *carefully* made, with an eye to detail; made for his/its own sake, not just for profit. Maybe I am stretching a point, but I can imagine the painter giving each clown an individuality, and as she does so flying away in her imagination from the monotony of ordinary life.

My quick definition of a miracle is 'a situation where God's personality shines through', and I think God's love shines through in this 'postcard' of the clown. I see in him three things: the wonder of creation, love as the source of creative energy, and the triumph of hope over adversity. Each of these is an aspect of God's personhood. I know it's easy to bandy the word *love*, but you might say that God's self-giving love is the Big Bang at the centre of the theological enterprise; all aspects of theology are like beams radiating out from this central explosion of meaning, and miracles are those radiating beams.

But does the clown bear any relation to biblical miracles? Surely a distinction has to be made between an ordinary, explicable toy and supernatural events such as the raising of Lazarus, the stilling of the storm, changing water into wine, and the numerous miracles of healing. These are events to be wondered at, and don't happen like that any more.

Several points can be made in response. First, amazing

things still do happen which come as a surprise in the rational world of cause and effect. For example, people sometimes recover inexplicably from illness contrary to their doctors' expectations.

Second, in St John's Gospel miracles are not known as 'wonders', but as 'signs' of the glory of God – signs which point beyond themselves to a more subtle truth. Thus, the Feeding of the Five Thousand has more to do with interpersonal relationship, and with Jesus being the 'Bread of Life' who mediates the personality of God, than it does with thousands of people being filled on a mere five loaves. Similarly, other miracles have symbolic significance in addition to the amazement factor: the healing of the blind, the deaf, and the lame were signs which exactly fulfilled what the prophets had said would happen at the coming of the messiah; the various feeding miracles have eucharistic significance; and the stilling of the storm raises the very important question of *who* Jesus is – 'who is this that even the wind and the waves obey him?' implying the answer: the Son of God, 'through whom all things were made'.

Third, Jesus had a very ambivalent attitude towards miracles as *wonders*. From the outset he resisted the temptation to win converts by using miracles as entertainment, yet, on the other hand, God's power had to be evident in his ministry if people were to be convinced. Thus, while a miracle of healing can be dramatic, he sees it as essentially discreet – something which is discerned by faith, and not to be gossiped about. For example, when he cured a deaf man with a speech impediment, he took him aside privately, and when the healing was complete charged him to tell no one (Mark 7.32–6). But Jesus' audience was chronically sceptical, and repeatedly asked for signs as proof that he was who he said he was, or who they thought him to be. This he steadfastly refused to do. The Pharisees asked for a sign, and he replied, 'An evil and adulterous generation seeks for a sign'. He went on to suggest that the signs they were looking for were inherent to his way of life, and all would finally be revealed in his death and resurrection.

Fourth, miracles in the Bible are not unique to Jesus. In response to her selfless hospitality, Elijah provided a widow of Zaraphath with a cruse of oil which would never run dry, and a jar of meal which would never be spent. It is an amazing story with the deeper meaning that self-giving hospitality will bring endless fulfilment. In the early Church, the Apostles continue a ministry of miraculous healing, as when Peter heals the lame beggar at the Gate Beautiful: 'I have no silver and gold,' he says, 'but I give you what I have. In the name of Jesus Christ of Nazareth, walk.' This is the universe coming alive in a personal sort of way.

So I am claiming that the miracle of the clown is of the same species as the biblical miracles, and that God is no less active in the questions that the clown poses than he is in the question, 'Who is this that even the winds and waves obey him?' In both, the personality or personhood of God shines through.

At more sophisticated levels than my clown, art sees the potential hidden in the physical and personal relationships of the observed world, and the potential of materials to symbolize them visually. Art seems to be saying, 'Look, there is a better way'. And what it is showing us is that God's creativity is not only concerned with the creation of matter, but more importantly with realizing the *personal potential* intrinsic to being and matter.

Mother and Child

An actual postcard from the Yale University Art Gallery illustrates this. It is of Picasso's *First Steps* of 1943. The painting shows a woman with a triangular face, and all the familiar distortions that he used at that time, bending over an unattractively self-confident child making its first ungainly efforts to walk. The woman's face shows completely devoted attention to the child who has his back to her and wishes to stride away from her, dazzled and enthralled by the wonder of the world. It is a poignant picture about the tension between dependence and letting go in the parent/child relationship, and it establishes in the observer a shared humanity with, and affection for, these very ordinary people who, in real life, may not have been noticed at all. Who indeed are they? Could this mother and child caught in this crucial moment of development be the Virgin Mary and Christ? Whoever they are, it is a picture about the sacrament of relationship, in which a child's first steps become a holy mystery for his mother (and for God?), and we *behold* it. Picasso reveals a truth that has been staring us in the face all the time, and he has done it through strikingly imaginative and daring visual imagery. The gift of the artist to us is to help us to see what we immediately recognize, but had not previously seen for ourselves. This is a miracle.

Beside the Seaside

The theologian Ian Ramsey[1] called this instant of recognition the moment when the 'penny drops', and all is revealed. It is his own seaside postcard to us, conjuring up a picture of walking down the pier, looking into a dark viewfinder, putting your penny in the slot, and when it falls – seeing what the butler saw. It is a naughty card for a serious religious idea.

Being more philosophical about it, he says that a religious disclosure is 'a situation which has "depth" and "mystery"', something *more* than what is seen; and he thinks that such disclosures are likely to be characterized by odd events and odd language – or in Picasso's case, odd pictures. So 'oddity' has a distinctive theological importance. A good New Testament example is the story of the Road to Emmaus, where despite walking with the risen Christ for several miles, the disciples fail to recognize him. Only when he breaks bread at supper does the penny drop. The oddity comes next: as soon as they recognize him, he *vanishes out of their sight*. You would have thought that they might have had some explanations, or made some plans. But the very oddness says that there is much more to this than meets the eye. Which is just what I am saying about the clown and the Picasso.

One of Ramsey's own pictures of a penny-dropping miracle concerns the difficult theological idea of God's 'immutability' or changelessness. What kind of *human* situation can make sense of such an obscure idea? Suppose you meet a friend, he suggests, after a gap of twenty years; so much about him has changed – his face is lined, he stoops a little, he seems so much more serious than when you were students together. But then you realize that not *everything* about him has changed. Very soon that old bond of friendship is rekindled, and you realize that there is an essence to this friendship that has remained constant despite the ravages of time. This speaks of 'immutability', of values which last. 'So does immutability lead us to God, for it is in situations such as this that people have spoken of "seeing God" in their love for a friend.'[2]

All these examples are occasions when the universe comes alive in a personal way, and Christianity is in no way diminished if the penny has dropped in a secular rather than a religious context. In fact, on the contrary, Christianity is expanded whenever someone links their experience to the gospel narrative, because they are allowing the story to enter a critical dialogue with experience – which is precisely what God does through the life of Christ.

The penny is likely to drop in almost any circumstance where a person is reminded of things that matter deeply: in a relationship, new or renewed; in a crisis or tragedy; in parenthood; in separation; in a simple act of kindness; hearing a piece of music; in an everyday occurrence freshly observed; reading the Bible, a poem, or a novel.

When Philip Larkin was Chairman of the Booker Prize

committee in 1977, he said in his speech announcing the winner that he asked himself four questions about the novels he had had to read: 'Could I read it? If I could read it, did I believe it? If I believed it, did I care about it? And if I cared about it, what was the quality of my caring, and would it last?'[3] When a novel makes you care about it in this way, I think it is putting you in touch with a reality beyond the symbols of its words and sentences. In whatever frame of mind you started to read the book, it engages you more deeply than you expected, and by the end it has added another personal dimension to your experience which alters the way you see things, and therefore demands commitment.

Such an experience may afterwards be understood as directly religious, or simply as having contributed to your accumulated sense of what really matters. In either case it is an example of how miracles of revelation occur in non-specifically religious situations, where the underlying 'Christliness' of creation shines through. This, surely, is what George Herbert was getting at in his poem *The Elixer*:

> A man that looks on glass,
> On it may stay his eye;
> Or if he pleaseth, through it pass,
> And then the heaven espy.

When people say they are bored with religion, or can no longer see its relevance, perhaps they are saying that they have ceased to experience disclosure, or to see beyond the symbols. It no longer comes alive for them. This is particularly true of disillusioned young teenagers who, when they discover that the symbols they had accepted as real in childhood are in fact two-dimensional, dismiss them as superstitious nonsense, without being able to glimpse the reality they represent. However, exposure to Christian ideas in childhood, even if those ideas are subsequently rejected, provides a vocabulary in which to express the seriousness and commitment evoked in later years by the disclosure experiences of, for example, love, childbirth, parenthood, bereavement – these points of major transition which so often seem to demand the word 'God'.

God in the Atom

I said at the beginning of Chapter One that, because you can't write much on a postcard, many people think them essentially superficial missives. As I ponder the imponderable – the origin of the personal – I am tempted to agree. Although, I suppose Einstein might have sent a postcard simply saying '$E = mc^2$'. Then you would have had the special theory of relativity on a postcard!

A superficial look at the history of our planet would suggest that it is fundamentally impersonal. For nearly all its four and a half billion year history there has been no personal life on the earth, because there has been no *human* life on earth. So we have to ask ourselves whether this phenomenon, 'the personal', developed in the last hundred thousand years as human beings evolved? Or whether human beings, with their superior brain-power, slowly came to recognize and understand something that was already there which they called 'personal'?

It is hard to think that the physical universe is entirely neutral to values and meaning, because it is by contemplating the marvels of nature that many people have been persuaded of the existence of God. Gerard Manley Hopkins articulates this when he says that 'The world is charged with the grandeur of God', like an electric current; and that no matter how much human activity obscures God's grandeur, there is nevertheless 'the dearest freshness deep down things' which has to do with the Holy Spirit brooding 'over the bent world'.

A student told me that when she's standing in church she feels like she's on a mountain top or by the sea. 'I am taken beyond myself,' she said. 'I believe that in the universe there's a bias towards life and goodness; and this is what I call God, but I am not sure that I understand much of what the Church teaches.' She had seen beyond the symbolism of perpendicular architecture into the transcendent, leaping aspiration that it signifies, and had linked this with the religious sense of awe sometimes experienced on a high mountain. It is no accident that many of the biblical encounters with God occurred on a mountain top: Moses on Sinai, Elisha and the chariots of fire, the transfiguration of Jesus, and Jesus going into the hills to pray.

In the eighteenth century it was thought that the universe was designed and set in motion by God, rather as a clockmaker designs a clock, and that the mechanical balance of everything in nature implied a designer who must be God. The Big Bang and Darwinism changed all that – the universe is expanding, not fixed, and if species evolved, they couldn't have been designed. However, the instinctive view that God is evident in nature won't go away. It might have something to do with the inventiveness of nature, its evolutionary prodigality, as if nature were expanding her own repertoire before our very eyes in a virtuoso performance of infinite potential; but it also has to do with the intuitive sense, made famous by Plato, that what we experience here on earth is a reflection of a transcendent and brilliant reality of truth and values elsewhere.

For Christians this transcendent reality is the personal God, who is known in Jesus Christ. And this very event of God's becoming human is a miracle which testifies to the underlying personal nature of the world. That is the significance of St John's claim that in the beginning was the Word, and that 'all things were made through him' (John 1.3).

What this means for theology is that religious disclosure taps into the underlying personal (Godly or Christly) nature of creation. At first glance the physical world may seem dry and impersonal, but personal value actually pervades the whole of creation. If all we know and experience has developed out of the original Big Bang; if everything has emerged from the gases of that massive nuclear explosion, then the creatures who have experienced and recognized the 'personal' have also emerged from that very creative energy, and it could be said that such values are innate to creation itself.

You might object that I am defining God too narrowly as 'personal', because the model for what is 'personal' is limited humanity itself. Are we trying to make the infinite God in our own image, rather than the other way round? What I am getting at is that in this astonishing universe, there is some quality which makes matter meaningful. If we were no more than gene machines relentlessly working to maximize life possibilities for the particular cells that make up our bodies, then what is the point of living? We might as well stop bothering. But we know that in the strange genetic process, meanings emerge – such as love, compassion, caring, beauty, and grace – which defiantly refuse to be dismissed as mere biological ploys used by the gene machine, but instead intimate God.

I am not saying that God is 'only personal', because I know that any single image is too simplistic, and that is why the next chapter considers the downside of imagery.

CHAPTER 4

THE LIMITS OF IMAGERY

> We are at best seekers of truth blundering on the edges of infinity.[1]
>
> Keith Ward

Taking the lid off the image repertoire is always asking for trouble. I received a deputation from some persons of the inclusive language variety who wished to amend the Nicene creed by deleting the word 'men' in the clause, 'for us men and for our salvation'. I suggested that next time the order of service was reprinted this should be considered, but they persisted and offered to scrub out the offending word with their black pens. No sooner was this done than other persons began to object. First there was the linguistic objection that 'men' was already an inclusive term, as in the Latin *homo* and the Greek *anthrōpos* – a generic word including both men and women. Then there was the 'who hath authority to tamper with the creed?' argument, which is a good argument if it is about Church authority, but a poor one if it is a way of saying that doctrine is fixed and can never develop. Then there was a much subtler argument: if you take away the word 'men', who is the 'us' that is left? Is it just we who are saying the creed in this service; is it just those who say the creed, in general; or is it all human beings? In other words, have you, by a well-intentioned politically correct act designed to include women, excluded a far greater number of the human race from Christ's saving work – namely, all those who don't call themselves Christians? Has the creed in its new form actually enshrined the 'them' and 'us' attitude that is the curse of the modern Church, and the greatest enemy of the gospel?

THE LIMITS OF IMAGERY

What this story shows is that language and imagery does not always increase understanding, but can be constrictive, particularly where it is only relevant to a particular culture, or only to certain people – in this case, men rather than women. I wish that the English language did distinguish more effectively between 'man' as human male person, and 'human being' as inclusive of women and men; it would make theology and worship much easier. How for instance are we to imagine God – as She, He or It? I try to avoid the personal pronoun wherever possible in relation to God because it is plain to me that God is beyond gender, despite the dominant male images of the Bible: Father, King, Lord, etc. You might object that God is always reduced by images whether physical or verbal, and that was why the Jews abhorred graven images, and would not even speak the sacred name of Yahweh, but substituted Adonai instead, because they didn't want to diminish God by tainting him with language. In any case, Yahweh was not in essence male, but pure 'being', derived from the verb 'to be' – 'I AM THAT I AM' (Exodus 3.14).

So surely the reality of God is too big for any particular attempt at imagery. In one sense yes, of course, but in another very important sense, no. How else is God to be apprehended by the finite human mind? The central plank of Christian theology, the incarnation, is God's great image self-projection. God becomes *man* in Jesus Christ – that much image limitation can't be avoided – although, interestingly, St Anselm entitles his great work about the atonement, *Cur Deus Homo*, not *Cur Deus Vir*, which means 'why did God become *inclusively human?*' rather than 'why did God become *a particular man?*'.

A Postcard from South London

This question of how imagery can be exclusive and narrowing, particularly where it is only relevant to certain people, is the subject of my next postcard, which I send to you from South

London. You might say that I picked it up from a church bookstall – in one of those privately printed editions.

It was a cold day. Many parts of the country were cut off by snow. On a Pennine road lorry drivers, their vehicles sunk in drifts, were filmed behind steamed-up windscreens. A farmer who had slipped into five feet of snow while trying to reach his sheep survived the night in a makeshift igloo scooped out with his bare hands. But in London we had woken to a mere sprinkling of white, just enough to emphasize the drabness of the winter townscape, dirty brick and too-small gardens back to back.

Children running through the churchyard threw slush at one another, scraped from the ground with saturated woollen gloves. One of these missiles, misdirected, hit Nicky on the side of the face. His reaction was abnormally slow. Stoically he wiped away the dribbling ice. Immediately the other boys stopped in their tracks, exchanged guilty glances, and silently dropped their ammunition. Nicky is blind.

At seven being blind is not a crisis. There is still so much to learn, so much instinctive optimism, so many skills to acquire, that you can consider yourself just a late developer in the art of seeing.

It was the second Sunday in Advent, and I had been invited to speak in this South London church, built in 1815 as a preaching shop rather than a theatre for sacramental mystery. Now the galleries have been dismantled, and an industrial heater, like a great blow lamp unequal to its task, roars in the cavernous space. The congregation, muffled and wrapped like carol singers on a Christmas card, arrived late and seated themselves sparsely around the pews, while servers and musicians flapped about as if knocking together a meal for guests who had turned up unexpectedly.

Icy fingers and makeshift ritual. This could be the worship of people on the move, arctic explorers, pilgrims, or even, in the time of Caesar Augustus, families travelling each to their own city to be enrolled.

THE LIMITS OF IMAGERY

Three-quarters of the way through the service, at the offertory, the second candle in the Advent ring was to be lit by one of the children. Nicky had been chosen, and so he came forward, taper in hand, flanked by two other boys, a year or two older, who led him to the table where the wreath stood. One of the sighted boys grasped Nicky's right hand and, overcoming his resistance, guided the taper to light the candle. I noticed that the blind boy turned his head away as if cowering from the flame. Then I realized that he was directing not his eyes but his ear to it. Could he actually hear what he was doing, I wondered – the tiny crackle of flame?

Afterwards, at the vicarage, people had been invited back to meet the preacher over sherry. These included a nun, a herbalist, the churchwarden, a barrister, and others I had not yet been introduced to. We sat in groups around the room making Sunday lunchtime chat. When Nicky entered, I was on the edge of a sofa discussing education with a teacher who had been one of the first male Fellows of Girton College, Cambridge.

His arrival stopped all conversation. Standing centre stage like a child about to play blind man's buff, he was introduced by devoted and delightful parents. Then came a bombardment of voices from all corners of the room: 'Hello, Nicky', 'How are you Nicky?', 'Nicky, I'm Eric. Remember?' As people spoke they stretched out their hands to touch him.

What did the child make of us? Could he disentangle the knot of voices, and did he welcome the hands-on approach? We were, besides, only trying to show human warmth, without the benefit of a visible smile. At first I recoiled from what seemed like competitive compassion, but later I realized that we had been spontaneous and generous, and if as a group we had been gauche, it was because we were frustrated by our impotence to do more. Which one of us, if we could have healed him, would not have spat on the ground and made a paste and wiped it on his eyes? We need not have worried. Our corporate bungling seemed no more than misplaced self-consciousness when he said, 'Where's the cat? I want to hold the cat.'

Then Sister Whoever-it-was decided to demonstrate her pastoral skill. So she gets up and takes Nicky by the hand and guides it to her girdle, which is knotted like a kind of brail. 'Remember this, Nicky?' she asks. 'Pull the rope and see (see?) if you can hear the bell ring?' Instinctively he recognized her kindness and set-apartness, which justifies such holy soppiness, and he played along. If only he could have raised his eyebrows and directed a knowing glance to his parents.

While the two of them were absorbed in their party trick, I stared at the two craters in his young face. The skin around them was delicate and tender, a soft, translucent tissue, revealing the opaque lacework of slender blood vessels beneath. In the pits of his eyes were wrinkled eyelids, small and defensive, that seemed to flinch. He didn't face the kindly nun, but turned an ear towards her.

We talk about compassion, but do we ever contemplate the inner space of blindness? I mean really imagine what it is like to stumble about in that dark room searching for the windows which we cannot find, hearing a world outside, but unable to be astonished by its bright colours.

'He loves music,' said his mother. 'In fact music has to be rationed, or he'll do nothing else. Beethoven is his favourite, isn't it, darling?'

'Well, Beethoven wrote his last great masterpieces when blind,' said the churchwarden.

'Will you play something for us on the piano?' I asked. Nicky could speak most effectively through the keyboard on which he had a prodigious talent, including the remarkably mature ability to imitate the style of different composers.

When Nicky had wandered, like a sleepwalker, from the room to be with the other children, his mother said to me, in a campaigning sort of way, that she had a bone to pick with me about my sermon. Despite the gentleness of her manner I knew at once that the attack was sure-footed, and that she

THE LIMITS OF IMAGERY

would not easily be appeased. It was the imagery she did not like. 'The people that walked in darkness have seen a great light: those who dwell in the land of deep darkness, on them has the light shone.'

'I think you were wrong,' she said, 'to talk of Jesus only as a light in darkness. What can that mean for someone like Nicky?'

'But he lit the Advent candle,' I replied.

'He doesn't enjoy lighting candles, he likes blowing them out,' she said defiantly.

What could I say to this convincing argument? I suggested that there are many ways of trying to understand the mystery of Christ's coming into the world, and the image of the dawn light or rising sun is only one of them. If there had been a Beethoven in the ancient world, the Bible might equally have spoken of Advent as a progression from silence to music. The people who walked in silence have heard a great sound.

'Yes, yes, yes,' she said excitedly. 'You are right.'

Nicky's blindness not only exposes the potential inadequacy of particular images, it also shows the danger of fixing on specific metaphors as the 'correct' interpretation of a spiritual truth, because by doing so some people are inevitably going to be excluded. On *reflection* one *sees* that a vast amount of Christian imagery refers to *darkness* and *light*, and the progress from one to the other, and that these symbols will be read in completely different ways by those who are blind and those who can see. It is little surprise, therefore, that the messianic vision of the future was one in which every human being would have all their faculties available with which to perceive God: 'Then the eyes of the blind shall be opened, and the ears of the deaf unstopped; then shall the lame man leap like a hart, and the tongue of the dumb sing for joy' (Isaiah 35.5–6). But for the time being we live with the partial revelation of the present.

Images and symbols by definition do not tell the whole story. At their most creative they reveal facets of truth from fresh angles, but when they lose their reference point they become like *The Hollow Men* of T. S. Eliot's poem, ideas without substance, of which he wrote, 'Between the idea/ And the reality ... Falls the shadow'.

All this convinces me that the Christian image repertoire needs to be as diverse as possible. Of course, Christian spirituality has recognized this, as is seen in the use of icons, music, silence, rosary beads, mantras, plays, architecture, and so on. But most of this is 'religious'. I want to extend the range of the image repertoire in all directions, so that Christ is not only the A–Z of language potential, but also the infra-red to ultraviolet of all visual potential, and the A major to G# minor of all music potential.

Nicky's story challenges me to broaden the scope of my journey into a different territory altogether – sound. And that is what I will try to do next.

CHAPTER 5

GOD IN MUSIC

> Awake, my lute, and struggle for thy part
>   With all thy art.
> The crosse taught all wood to resound his name,
>   Who bore the same.
> He stretched his sinews taught all strings, what key
> Is best to celebrate this most high day.'
>
> George Herbert, *Easter*

In Schaffer's play, *Amadeus*, Salieri fears that his rival, Mozart, has a direct line to God. Many others have heard the voice of God in music, including theologians such as the protestant Karl Barth, and the catholic Hans Küng. Even Einstein, hearing Menuhin play Beethoven, said, 'Now I know there is a God in heaven'. So what is it in music that is capable of opening up a new spiritual repertoire? Does music refer to meanings outside itself, or does it simply mean itself? George Steiner says starkly, 'Music means. It is brimful of meanings which will not translate into logical structures or verbal expression',[1] and he gives the example of Schumann, who when asked to explain a difficult *étude* sat down and played it a second time.[2]

Despite that warning, I want in this chapter to offer some 'postcards' which might give a clue to how music can bridge the gap between speechlessness and God.

The Botswana Bowyers

My starting point is an account of how music functions in one of the world's remaining primitive societies. At the climax of the story about his encounter in the Kalahari desert with the last surviving stone age men of Africa, Laurens van der Post describes the music of the Bushman.[3] The Bushman's ancient instrument is a long bow with a single string bound taut to the middle of the shaft. He beats the string with a stick, and holds one end of the bow to his open lips using his mouth as a sound box to amplify the music, like a jaws harp.

Thus the essential tool of his *survival* is also the source of his *music*. In the day he would kill a buck or a wildebeest with poisoned arrows from his bow, and in the evening he would make music on his bow-instrument, 'hunting meaning in the wasteland of sound', as van der Post poetically puts it.

He goes on to observe that music played on such stringed instruments expressed both contentment and thanks for life. At the end of the day the small community would sit round listening to one of their number playing the therapeutic music, which brought calm and peace to their faces.

On a particular occasion, when out hunting, he tells of meeting a group of Bushmen who literally were dying of thirst in the fiery desert, not having drunk for days. After they had been given water from the explorers' supply, the first thing they did was to produce a lyre and make music as a way of saying thank you.

However, the greatest musical occasions he describes were those of the dance. To the author's surprise they had no drums, but created rhythm by the clapping of cupped hands and the beating of their feet on the ground. This provided the backing for the notes of the single-string bow, and the primitive four-stringed lyres, played by the women. One such dance occurred when, with the help of twentieth-century guns, the hunters had brought home a mighty bull eland, a greatly prized and symbolic beast. Another happened at the coming of the rains. Music was inextricably linked with survival. He concluded, therefore, that music was as vital as water, food, and fire – and I would add, religion.

Sometimes we forget how recent our civilization is and that

our inherited genetic coding does not have to reach back very far to connect with our primitive forebears – there are many programmes deep in the psyche codified from experience. If, in a country where there are no dangerous spiders, many of us suffer from inherited arachnophobia, and if it is true that we look at sunlight on the seashore with such pleasure because we have a distant memory of emerging from the waters of the earth on to the dry land, then it would scarcely be surprising if music put us in touch with primitive ancestral memories of thanksgiving under the stars for survival in a hostile environment, and the contentment of family, and tribal solidarity.

The benefits of survival and social cohesion are central features of the Judaeo/Christian tradition, for which God receives appropriate praise and thanksgiving in the worship of synagogue and church. In the Old Testament God is the deliverer (from Egypt, from the Philistines) who ensures the survival of his people. In the New Testament Christ offers a new life, which transcends and survives even death. These values are embodied in the covenant of the Old Testament, St Paul's idea of the Church as the Body of Christ, and in the heavenly communion of saints.

Survival, thanksgiving and social cohesion: at first they seem thoroughly selfish responses, but they are also to do with human beings reaching out to God in extreme conditions and recognizing their weakness and smallness in the vast wonder of God's creation. This was the vision of Job as he saw a God who could bind the cluster of the Pleiades and loose Orion's Belt, and whose awesome wonder eventually reduced Job to silence, and to repent in dust and ashes (Job 42.3–6). If music is able to express something of that, then that is the first clue to the power of its spiritual meaning.

Amadeus himself

A second clue is what is known by critics as music's *form* – how it is constructed. Despite Steiner's comment that music is brimful of meanings that will not translate, music can nevertheless be analysed, and broken down into its component parts. It is a kind of 'language', the 'grammar' of which can be learnt. An example of such 'grammar' is the 'sonata' form, which has influenced so much instrumental music in the last four centuries.

Mozart seemed to have had an intuitive mastery of form, evident in the way his music creates the brilliantly unexpected, while at the same time sounding perfectly natural, as if it were meant to be. Hence, perhaps, the sense that God is revealed, because God is original, unexpected, yet perfect in being, the 'I am' behind all creation.

This is an idea which seems to me to have a lot in common with the view put forward by some mathematicians and scientists, that the more elegant, or beautiful, a theory is, the more likely it is to be true.[4] Music and mathematics have often been seen as related disciplines, and it is not difficult to see why, because at one level music is the physics of the interrelation of sound frequencies. The Oxford mathematician, Roger Penrose, believes that when the mind grasps a mathematical idea, it is making contact with an external Platonic world of mathematical concepts; that mathematical truth is as it were 'out there' waiting to be discovered. Similarly, you might argue that when people find God revealed in Mozart, they are saying that the composer has expressed a musical truth of such elegance that he has mediated unwittingly a truth that is 'out there'. In fact Penrose makes the connection between mathematics and art himself when he says that artists often feel 'that in their greatest works they are revealing eternal truths which have some kind of etherial existence.'[5]

Mozart: Traces of Transcendence is the elegant title of Professor Hans Küng's investigation into why Mozart's music provides many people with a sense of divine disclosure. He is at pains to acknowledge that such experience only comes to those who are open to it, and to avoid any suggestion that he is making a god out of Mozart, the man, who as is well known was no paragon of virtue and possessed a truly scatological sense of humour. A pivotal point in his argument is taken from Karl Barth: Küng says that Barth's great insight into the mystery of Mozart's music 'lies in the fact that it constantly makes audible both the light *and* the dark, joy *and* sorrow, life *and* death ... but the darkness is always transcended and done away with in the light'.[6] He goes on to quote from the *Church Dogmatics* where Barth says that in Mozart one hears 'the positive far more strongly than the negative'. In other words, Mozart expresses in sound what Psalm 23 expresses in words, 'Yea, though I walk through the valley of the shadow of death, I shall fear no evil, for thou art with me'.

Perfect or Interrupted Cadence?

This counter-balancing between light and dark, joy and sorrow, leads to a third clue, which is music's relation to the emotions. Whether it is the pulsating rhythm of a rock concert leading to feelings of ecstasy and exaltation, or hearing in the second movement of Beethoven's *Eroica* Symphony, the *Marcia Funebre*, sadness, despair or grief, there can be no doubt that music is capable of affecting the emotions. At the simplest level it is an idea expressed in the old cliché that minor keys express sadness, and major keys joy and triumph.

But it is more subtle than that, and the beginning of explanation lies in the way in which musical sounds, when placed in relation to each other, can create either dissonance or harmony. Press down two adjacent piano keys at once and they produce a clashing dissonance which jars the ear and cries out for some kind of resolution; press down two white keys that are separated by another white key (a third apart) and they produce a harmony which the ear is content to listen to. Project this simple example into the labyrinthine music of Bach, the Beatles, or Beethoven, and you find a complex of counter-flowing sounds which create in the listener a tension, sometimes of excitement, sometimes of anxiety, which can only be satisfied by musical resolution. It is a creative tension which, at its best, can work on the imagination in such a way as to be a parable for the experience of suspense, uncertainty and resolution in real life. Music can therefore be cathartic, cleansing the emotions and freeing the spirit. That is why one feels a sense of triumph at the end of a great symphony when the final sequence of cadences is repeated over and over again – tension, resolution, tension, resolution. It is as if to say all shall be well and all manner of things shall be well.

When I was taught basic harmony at school, one of the rudimentary rules was that the leading note (the 'te' of the tonic sol-fa scale) must always be resolved – don't leave the listener suspended in mid-air with that nagging anxiety that the music is unfinished. Just try singing up the tonic sol-fa scale and stopping at 'te' to see what I mean. Doh, re, me, fa, so, la, te ...

The psychological effect of music's exploration of dissonance and harmony ties in closely with one of the basic religious insights about God – namely, that God brings order out of chaos. Christ is the healer, the one who integrates the disintegrated lives of people such as the madman who lived amongst the tombs. Thus God is found in the restoration of order and the resolution of dissonance – physical, spiritual, emotional. 'In the beginning ... the earth was without form, and void' but God brought light and order (Genesis 1.1–3).

So far I have identified three aspects of the spiritual potential of music: a primitive link with survival, the eternal beauty of form, and the resolution dissonance. Maybe this simply substantiates the view that musical meanings cannot translate into logical structures or verbal expression, and that it is a far too extravagant claim to say that God is revealed in music. I accept that. But nevertheless I hope I have already shown that music is part of the image factory which expands the spiritual repertoire. Such a claim is justified, I would have thought, on the grounds of music's historical record alone.

It is a particularly interesting record which backs up my thesis that Christ is sometimes experienced more vividly through secular imagery than specifically religious imagery. Music as we know it in Western culture has its origins very much in the worship of the Church, with the composition of music for the mass, and the evolution of the motet as a beautified setting of passages of scripture for use in worship. Composers relied on patronage for their living, and the princes of church and state competed with each other to keep up high standards. Thus musical ideas and techniques quickly cross-fertilized and mutated between the sacred and secular. A good example of this is the way in which some Mozart masses can sound almost too operatic and sensual to be used in worship, and how some of the most beautiful passages in his operas, particularly *The Magic Flute*, have a spiritual purity that one associates with the best of 'church' music.

Much religious music touches the sublime: Allegri's *Miserere*, Bach's *Matthew Passion*, Mozart's *Requiem*, and Purcell's *Funeral Anthems* are examples in my list. In these, words and music are combined together in such a way that the one offsets the other, and brings out meanings and emotions that would otherwise be hidden. However, it is hard to resist the thought that these works are transcended by the great symphonies and concertos, that are in some sense their progeny, even more refined creatures, capable of enlarging the spiritual imagination without the use of words. Such music can bridge the gap between speechlessness and God in a way which necessarily defies explanation. And perhaps we should be grateful for that.

So I am not trying to promote an absolutist argument. I accept the objection that the meaning given to music is largely a matter of subjective judgement, culturally determined, depending on what ideas and images you bring to the musical experience. I went to the crematorium to conduct the funeral of a very grand old lady. The organist, who thought I was new, fussed around me in a Jeevesish sort of way, and began to tell me where to sit and how to press the button – 'right in the middle, not at the sides, or it won't *engage*'. When I looked over his shoulder at the piece of music he planned to play, I read, 'From the Suite in D – HAMLET CIGARS'. This piece of Bach, then, was considered suitable to accompany in the coffin, *and* to advertise a certain brand of cigar. Perhaps it was a subliminal government health warning: 'smoking can damage your health.'

On another occasion an English professor told me he was outraged to discover one of his undergraduates plugged into pop music while reading Shakespeare. How, he asked himself, could the student study a serious writer with all that pandemonium being pumped into his brain? Subsequently he found himself asking another question: whether he would have felt differently if the music had been Mozart? You see, the professor felt there was a congruity between Shakespeare and Mozart, related to artistic merit, and an incongruity between Shakespeare and pop music related to what he considered depth versus triviality. But the fact that the professor questioned his initial prejudice shows that he knew this was a subjective judgement, and that of course there is good pop music, just as there is bad classical music.

But it is not all subjectivity, not just images from our own culture being played back to us – music is a self-sufficient language of its own. It was in a church service that I first heard music played on the gamelan, a Balinese instrument constructed of tuned metal plates over brightly coloured wooden resonating tubes, played with hammers, a bit like a xylophone. The music, which was entrancingly rhythmic and syncopated with persistent and repetitive tonal patterns, had no cultural meaning for me, except that it sounded 'eastern', yet I thought it was the most impressive and spiritual part of a service which otherwise was extremely wordy.

An Instrument of Four Strings

The intrepid traveller in the world of music will not only be keen to visit all the concert halls she can, she might want to know more about how the miracle is achieved. Maybe she enquires about the composer's life: the things that influenced him, his passions, hates, psychology. Or she attends a class given by the performer. She might be fascinated by the evolution of musical instruments, and therefore how musical performances have changed as technology has improved. She might visit a museum to see their collection of viols, and crumhorns, and bamboo pipes.

Here is one of those rather 'arty' cards, like the ones you buy in museums and libraries, depicting an artefact or ancient manuscript, often used by refined people to engrace their minor communications and thank you letters. Printed at the bottom of the picture in fine letters are the words, *The Violoncello*.

This box wants to speak. Even as it is taken out of its case it receives a knock and complains with a short, hollow shudder. Once I read a story about a young man who was teaching a stone to talk – a project which, as you can guess, came to nothing – but it gave the writer a theme for reflection, and the memorable line, 'Nature's silence is its one remark'. But this box wants to speak. Which is a more promising start.

It is after all little more than a wooden box – a right shapely box, to be sure, with the grace of a young woman – a box with strings drawn tightly over a vertical bridge which stands three-quarters of the way down its curvaceous belly. If we vibrate the strings with a horsehair bow, the sound which issues is like the first primitive grunt of inarticulate speech. With practice and experiment this noise is refined into a note, a sound with shape and meaning. You can sing the note out loud if you want, to prove that it exists. Now press down your finger on one of the strings and you get another note – different in tonal character, less harsh – and by vibrating the finger backwards and forwards on the string the note is tempered into emotion.

Music must have been made on stringed instruments ever since man first held a piece of gut between his teeth and twanged it, but no one thought to vibrate the strings of his harp with a bow until the tenth century, somewhere in central Asia, where they were very good bowyers. Soon the practice spread through the Muslim world and into Europe; and, in medieval painting, angels began to appear playing their heavenly music on rebecs – beautiful pear-shaped instruments held on the thigh. This bass instrument of the violin family is held upright between the legs of the seated player.

Taught by Tortelier

My favourite musical postcard, however, is of the late, great Paul Tortelier and his beautiful cello with its famous angled spike. Wisps of grey hair fly backwards as man and instrument fuse in an ecstatic dance; his aquiline face stares out into the high space of the auditorium as if inspiration comes from beyond.

I had asked him to give a lecture recital entitled 'Music and Spirituality', but he said it was impossible to give a systematic explanation of how music and faith intersect; however, he was willing to give a master-class to three students instead, and the audience would have to make their own connections.

On the night, it seemed curious that a packed house should be spellbound by the laborious process of teaching – all stops and starts, apologies and repeats. Wouldn't it be better to come back later when the rehearsals were over, and hear Boccherini, Brahms, and Tchaikovsky played in concert performance? But the lure of going behind the scenes is in many senses even more fascinating than the concert itself, because we are getting an intimate glimpse of the human side of the artist, stripped of all the glitz and glamour of the concert platform. In principle, the artist is a magician who wants you to see only what she wants you to see. Perhaps, with false humility and sleight of hand, she pretends that the process of making and invention is uninteresting and dull. But we, the voyeurs, know that it is not. We are all agog. Give us as much detail as you can.

The three student cellists who bravely volunteered to be the subjects of this class varied in ability from high school to concert standard. The result was that we were taken through the entire range of technical problems, from something as basic as how to hold the bow, to the finer subtleties of interpretation. I repeatedly asked myself why it so difficult for the apprentice to imitate the master, and couldn't resist the thought that this is a theological question of some importance.

The art of bowing, which looks so simple, is much more complicated than it seems. Which *part* of the bow should you use; how much of its length is needed for this phrase or that note; what weight should be exerted on the string; how do you start without a scratch? (Every parent would be glad to know this.) The bow is placed on the string exerting some pressure, and as the note is played the pressure is released. The exasperated pupil tries this twenty times, but cannot get it right, whereas Tortelier makes a beautifully clean melodic sound with a single stroke of the bow, every time, without fail. His eyes look quizzically, sympathetically – can you do it like this? Can you do it like this?

'In my garden there are two beautiful turtle doves,' he says. 'When they fly together they fly in perfect harmony, *comme ça*' (he flutters his hands in the air). 'You must make your playing like those doves, *oui?*'

'A musician is a sculptor, like Rodin; a painter, like Botticelli, Cézanne, or Rembrandt; a thinker – how do you say, *philosophe*? – a lover, a dancer, and a sportsman.' He falls to the ground and does some press-ups. The audience applauds loudly, excited by the charismatic energy of the man. The lesson has become a performance by the teacher. The pupil, on whom so much attention had just been focused, suddenly feels like a spare part, and embarrassedly joins in the applause too – like a contestant outshone by a game show host.

He continues, 'I do not play like the baroque players, da da da da da da. They play like that because they cannot play the cello! Do not try to be a purist. Jesus Christ was not a purist – he was pure – but he was not a *puriste*. He would play with freedom,' (he plays some Bach) 'but not too free;' (he plays with extravagant rubato) 'this is sentimental. In all things not too much, but just enough.'

When Tortelier said that Christ was not a purist, I think he must have had in mind both his impatience with pharisaism, and his eye for the essence of a moral question, rather than its formal structure. His playing was like healing on the sabbath day. Jesus said that the sabbath was made for man, not man for the sabbath. Applied to Bach, I suppose this would be: Bach was made for man, not for the baroque players.

'Maybe in a few years I will meet Bach,' he said cheekily. 'Maybe he will kick me. But I would rather be told by Bach how to play his music than by purists.' It was not to be a few years, but a few days. He died of a heart attack three weeks later!

The idea of Jesus playing the cello seemed neither blasphemous nor absurd – especially listening to the dissonant, interrogative, counterpoint of Bach. I was reminded of a poem by R. S. Thomas, *The Musician*,[7] which describes a recital by the violinist, Kreisler, who, he says,

> ... so beautifully suffered
> For each of us upon his instrument.

He goes on to compare the toil of the artist with the crucifixion of Christ:

> The hands bleeding, the mind bruised but calm,
> Making such music as lives still.

> And no one daring to interrupt
> Because it was himself that he played ...

George Herbert had used the same image three hundred years earlier when he wrote of Christ:

> He stretched his sinews taught all strings, what key
> Is best to celebrate this most high day.

Those lines from his poem *Easter* recognize that the *effort* and the *suffering* of Christ the artist are prerequisites of the music of Easter.

The most telling line of Thomas' poem is, 'because it was himself that he played', because it makes a connection between the manner in which God's love is incarnated through the passion of Christ, and the manner in which music is incarnated through the self-giving of the player. That is why there is a significant difference between a performance on CD, however good, and a live performance: seeing the music being incarnated, as well as hearing its sound, adds an extra dimension, and potentially expands the image repertoire. In his poem, Thomas says that he arrived at the recital late and had to sit on the stage,

> So near that I could see the toil
> Of his face muscles, a pulse like a moth
> Fluttering under the fine skin,
> And the indelible veins of his smooth brow.

Its brilliant metaphor of the incarnation is my fourth, and most important, aspect of the spiritual potential of music.

This discussion had started with the claim that Christ was not tied down to the dead letter of the law, but then, with rabbinic skill, Tortelier turned his image of freedom round on itself: 'A musician is not free; you are a slave.' Then, rhetorically to one of the students, 'Are you free *not* to play the cello?

Of course you are not. Are you free when you practise your scales? Are you free when you play in a string quartet? You must play with the others, you must be all together.' It was as if he had picked up the paradox of Christian freedom expressed in the mattins collect, 'whose service is perfect freedom', or in Christ's teaching that whoever would save their life must first lose it. Playing is a vocation which demands discipline if it is to be fulfilling.

The final sentence of Tortelier's obituary in the *Guardian* said that 'His belief in the beneficent power of music as a vital force for good never wavered.' One of the pieces being studied in the master-class was Tchaikovsky's *Rococo Variations*. At one point he stopped the student playing and said, 'Music is about love, (pronounced not *luv*, but *lovv-e*). Musicians are lovers (*lovveurs*). And gentleness. The world needs more gentleness, *non?*' As he speaks I can't help noticing the callouses on the fingertips of his left hand, like the pads of a dog's paw, hardened by eight hours practice a day. The *Variations* continue: 'Two people dance together. They are married – but not to each other! They wish they were free to marry, but they are not. Come to me, come to me. No I cannot, no I cannot. Then at last, goodbye.'

'Everything is in curves and lines – look at the architecture of this church. Keppler, the astronomer, says music matches the created order: 7 notes in a scale – 7 days in a week; 12 semitones in the scale – 12 hours in the day; 24 keys – 24 hours in the day . . .' Is this theology, or is it a bogus science of coincidental numbers? I think of the student who asked to be confirmed because she found traces of God's transcendence in the perpendicular architecture of my church. This is the incarnational ache all over again – the raw spiritual experience – this time answered by music.

The class was almost over when Tortelier turned to the audience and said in his drawling French accent, 'Everything I say is banal. My wife tells me, Paul, everything you say is banal – it's the way you say it.'

Then he takes up his cello, adjusts his bow, and without any further comment plays a Bach sonata, and you realize how all the techniques he has explained and bullied over in the class are brought together into this captivating explosion of creation. He looks out at you with eyes bulging, almost mad, asking you the question: is this right? Isn't this the way it should be done? Every muscle is poised, every vein stands out; player and instrument are united. It is not a matter of effortless ease, this genius, it is a labour and a struggle, and a torment, even, that he 'so beautifully suffered for each of us upon his instrument'. At the end the man is exhausted having given all, and he relaxes as if it were the seventh day. Those who have been privileged to hear this recognize that they have heard something extraordinary because they have been in the workshop. They have seen the failure of an apprentice, but also they have seen that the master does not simply have as it were a God-given gift; his art has cost him discipline, love, and physical distress over many years, and the final product is not on show like a sparkling jewel, but pours from the sweat of his brow.

CHAPTER 6

MEETING GOD AT THE EDGE OF FAITH

> Extremes are not edges, and the edge is where he excels: the edge of comedy, the edge of respectability, the edge of despair.
>
> Alan Bennett on John Gielgud

'Then the devil took him to the holy city, and set him on the pinnacle of the temple, and said to him, 'If you are the Son of God, throw yourself down' (Matthew 4.5–6). The last chapter ended with a Bach sonata exquisitely played by Paul Tortelier. He excelled at the edge of cello playing and the edge of musical interpretation. His faith was also at the edge of religion, and I think he excelled at that too.

Christians need to accept that God is not met solely at the centre of religious language and institutions, but also at the edge, and they should be grateful for that liberation. Some people who have been to the centre need to end up at the edge, because they find the centre too intense or too clubby; and some at the edge can never get closer to the centre however much they try. Jesus himself seemed to have lived at the edge of formal religion, and found that people living at the edge of faith (in parables and in life) had often understood the kingdom of God better than the experts. It is this emphasis of the gospel story more than any other that makes Christianity a 'public' rather than a 'private' religion, because it is not merely for those who 'belong'.

Then there are those who are beyond the edge; not, as it were, in outer darkness, but having no vocabulary with which to connect with traditional theology. For example, I was asked to meet a class of fifteen-year-olds, doing an RE project, to give them a potted history of my particular church, where Thomas Cranmer had been tried for heresy, John Wesley had preached some of his most influential sermons, and John Henry Newman had promoted the 'Oxford Movement' – the nineteenth-century catholic revival in the Church of England. Not one of them had ever been to a church before. They hadn't got a clue. 'Altar', 'font', 'pulpit' meant nothing, let alone the niceties of theology. There was a complete culture gap which frightened me. My sermon text for the next day was, 'Other sheep I have that are not of this fold' (Jesus speaking in John 10.16), and I thought that these children's cultural alienation, being totally outside the Christian frame of reference, would be a good illustration. It occurred to me too that sheep, shepherds, pastors, and bishops' crooks are also images on the far side of the culture gap!

So I want to send a postcard of encouragement to all those who are attracted to God, but are not conventionally religious; people who stumble over bits of the creed, who don't like being herded, who are put off by organized religion or the hypocrisy of its practitioners, who feel unworthy, who think traditional ways are not the only ways to God, who have been to the centre and back again, or who are isolated from traditional Christianity by a culture shift over which they have no control. In short, most people. Approximately 70 per cent of people in Britain claim to believe in God, but only a very small proportion of these actually practises a particular 'faith'. May I therefore address this card to 'most people'? And say to more traditional Christians, of whom I count myself one, that those at the edge challenge us to stretch our imaginations, and travel outside the security of our institutions where we will find fresh insight into the person of Christ who is, besides, 'all and in all' (Colossians 3.11).

The first thing to remember is that Christianity is bigger than the Church, whatever the Church may tell you to the contrary. It is true that the fifth-century St Augustine of Hippo said there is no salvation outside the Church – *Salus extra ecclesiam non est* as he put it in his essay *Concerning Baptism* – but I am sure he was wrong. The Church is too vulnerable, and fragile, and fragmentary, and prone to mistakes to be the only vessel capable of holding salvation. Christianity is about universal principles embodied in Christ, the eternal Word, the A–Z of all language potential, and of all potential; whereas the churches are too often about local principles – communities and clubs which can get introspective and self-protective and small-time. This was as true in Augustine's day as it is today. His Church was dogged by infighting about whether you had to have morally pure clergy in order to have valid sacraments, and whether salvation could be earned or came as a free gift from God. Today's Church in the West is dogged by similar arguments about whether you have to have male priests in order to have valid sacraments, and whether salvation is for this chosen few or that chosen few. So it's always important to remember that Christianity is bigger than the Church, *and* bigger than any particular branch of it. Some people get round this criticism by holding an idealized view of the Church as a spiritual entity somewhere 'out there', which transcends all the follies of church politics and the vanities of its institutions, and they might argue it is mystically identical with Christ – but, to be honest, I don't find this helpful.

A Portrait of Graham 'Thomas' Greene

So you will not be surprised to discover that my picture on this postcard is not of a church or cathedral, but of a man who when he was baptized into the Catholic Church, took the baptismal name of Thomas – not after Thomas Aquinas, but after Thomas the Twin, otherwise known as 'Doubting' Thomas. Graham Greene wrestled with God at the borders of faith and the edge of the Church, and wrote about it in his novels. Both his personal *story* and his stories illustrate the spiritual dilemmas of those who live at the outer limits of faith, and those who have been to the centre, but need to end up at the edge. Indeed, it is from Greene that I get this idea of the 'edge', when he says that if he were to choose an epigraph for all the novels he had written, it would be from Browning's *Bishop Bloughram's Apology*: 'Our interest's in the dangerous edge of things'.[1] When asked what he meant by the dangerous edge of things, he described it as 'the narrow boundary between loyalty and disloyalty, between fidelity and infidelity, the mind's contradictions, the paradox one carries with oneself.'[2] It is an ambiguity which belongs in the world of spies and double-agents, about which he writes, but also to the world of religion — priests who are outwardly orthodox but secretly have lost their faith, and lay people who deny having any faith, but are hounded by it until they submit.

Two examples from his novels illustrate this. The first from *The Power and the Glory* (1940) which tells the story of a shabby 'whisky' priest in communist Mexico where the practice of religion has been outlawed. The nameless priest, who embodies human weakness, has many opportunities to escape to safety over the border, but repeatedly his residual Christian conscience stops him as he responds to the peasants' requests for the sacramental ministry that only he can give. Throughout the novel he is on the run — from the police, and from his religion. But God (or Roman Catholicism) hounds him until he is captured and put before the firing squad, where he finds, in some ragged sense, a martyr's crown, and good has had a marginal victory over evil.

The second is from *A Burnt-Out Case* (1960), where the central character, Querry, a famous architect, tries to expunge his previous life by escaping to a leper hospital in the Belgian Congo. Here he finds not only doctors and nurses, but the monks and nuns of a religious community, who remind him of 'an illness long forgotten' — his Christian faith. Dr Colin tells him, ' "You're too troubled by your lack of faith, Querry. You keep on fingering it like a sore you want to get rid of" '. But he can't get rid of it, and ironically, his personal qualities – kindness to his servant, and eventual commitment to building a new hospital – inspire a resurgence of faith within the community. He protests that he has been a hedonist and a womanizer and is not worthy of their esteem, but they lionize him as a new Albert Schweitzer. Eventually he is shot by one of his greatest admirers, the jealous Rycker, who thinks, quite mistakenly, that Querry is the father of his wife's child. It is another martyrdom.

These two figures reveal the fugitive experience of many at the edge – that weird sense of being hunted by God, rather than searching for the divine for yourself. It is an age-old experience beautifully captured in the poetry of Psalm 139,

> Whither shall I go from thy spirit?
> Or whither shall I flee from thy presence?
> If I ascend to heaven, thou art there!
> If I make my bed in Sheol, thou art there!

Or again in the nineteenth-century Francis Thompson's poem, *The Hound of Heaven*, which begins,

> I fled him down the nights and down the days;
> I fled him down the arches of the years;
> I fled him down the labyrinthine ways
> Of my own mind; and in the midst of tears ...

and ends with words spoken by the pursuer, the hounding love of Christ, 'Lo, all things fly thee, for thou fliest me!'

How much is there of Greene himself in these strange heroes? It never does to make simplistic identifications between writers and their fictions, but inevitably there are parallels. In the interview with Marie-Françoise Allain, he says that when he was converted to Rome from Anglicanism, he was attracted by the uninhibited dashes of bright colour thrown on the canvas of faith by a rich sacramentalism, verging, as he says, on magic and superstition. He adds perversely that he finds superstition and magic more 'rational' than such abstract ideas as the Holy Trinity, which is to say that those at the edge are likely to be less impressed by rational argument than by the kind of pictorial religion represented by, for example, Spanish baroque churches and the razzmatazz of colourful religious processions through the streets.

He speaks admiringly of a Spanish priest friend who, although not conventionally pious, seemed to have an absolute faith. When asked to describe his faith he said, 'I do not believe in God, I touch him.'[3] We are meant to recognize this intimacy with God as *real* and saintly; down-to-earth Mediterranean passion in contrast to the chill winds of Northern protestantism; experience versus rationality. And there is something in it. One thinks of the significance of touch for those in the gospels who were made whole by Christ: the woman with the issue of blood who touched the hem of his garment, the lepers healed by the laying-on of hands, and the man blind from birth whose eyes Jesus anointed with clay made with his own spittle. In *A Burnt-Out Case*, Doctor Colin's work in the leprosy mission is more significant sacramentally than intellectually: his 'notes had small value, but his fingers, he knew, gave the patients comfort: they realised they were not untouchable.'

Greene disparages Anglicanism as 'foggy', and does so in the same breath as he criticizes the rebel Catholic theologians Küng and Schillebeeckx. He says that 'Fr Schillebeeckx's declarations ... have suddenly revived in me a deep faith in the inexplicable, in the mystery of Christ's resurrection ... Don't you think there's something like a small miracle of grace there for we who are semi-lapsed?'[4] This advocacy of the expansion of the image repertoire through parable and picture, rather than rational, philosophical argument, is especially telling from an *outsider* because it suggests that if you lose the mystery, then you lose the appeal.

I am also intrigued by the idea of being 'semi-lapsed'. It means he wants to stand at a distance, and keep a foot in the door at the same time, because he has an underlying faith that refuses to go away. 'On the whole I keep my faith while enduring long periods of disbelief.'[5] Many people on the edge would identify with that, and I suspect many more in the mainstream of the Christian Church, if they were honest, would admit the same; and I wish they would because nothing blunts the cutting-edge of Christianity more than the keeping up of appearances, and pretending that it is improper to wrestle with belief.

But I don't intend to make a romantic hero out of Greene, or to bow to his opinions just because he was a famous novelist. Such people can become crafty old tyrants who use their lingeringly residual faith to justify reactionary posturing. Those who became famous for asking the questions, suddenly want no more questions asked. The literary ones are usually the worst. They want 'old' language: the Authorised Version and the Book of Common Prayer, or the Latin Mass, and they want it primarily for its aesthetic effect, its beauty and its resonance, and readily forgive the text whenever poor translation obscures the meaning. Beauty before meaning. They want a reconstructed literalism in which stories are taken at face value again. It is nostalgia, maybe, for the days when they actually believed, and they have never been able to accept that tradition not only moves, but *grows*. These are the sort who also want bishops to 'speak out' with terrible blimpish certainty. Although, to be fair, I imagine bishops speaking out was the last thing Greene wanted.

Second Thoughts

So you've received the Graham Greene postcard, then? As soon as I'd dropped it in the letterbox, I began to wonder if I'd done the right thing. So I am sending another by way of explanation. You see these days it is so easy to be misunderstood. It might be considered sheer perversity, in a religious book, to draw on the thoughts of a person who made himself an outsider – a sign of poor judgement, and bad taste, even infidelity. Why not seek God through the example of the saints, rather than through the writings of a self-confessed doubter? *Well* ... the Samaritan, the Prodigal Son, and the Unjust Steward immediately spring to mind as less than orthodox characters used by Jesus in his parables to exemplify the spiritual search. And, of course, Jesus did say that he came not to call the righteous, but sinners to repentance – a policy reflected in his choice of friends and disciples: Matthew the tax collector, Simon the Zealot, and Mary Magdalene to name but three.

But I do concede that the picture of Graham Greene is 'sepia' tinted, dating back to what seems now like an old-fashioned world. Things have changed, and are changing – faster than many people can keep up with. Now, as we are constantly reminded, we live in a much more fragmented society where the profusion of choice means an increase of edges and a blurring of margins; where anxiety about the future of work and the future of the environment lead to a corporate 'edginess', especially among the young.

This is the world of the fifteen-year-olds who had never been inside a church; where as many as one in three fifteen-year-old boys carry weapons to school; and where drugs are increasingly accepted as a leisure option. It is the 'post-modern' world of seismic culture shift in which the old certainties have disappeared, and widespread disillusion has set in with politics, religion, and traditional philosophical frameworks. 'Privatization' and 'deregulation' are bywords which apply not only to utility companies and buses, but to society in general. Marriage is deregulated – if you don't like it, get out; morality is deregulated, and many young people, as a *Guardian*/ICM poll[6] on the attitudes of children shows, 'are looking for figures of authority, someone or something they can trust and believe in', and they find it in their media lives –

cult brand identification, football teams, personalities ... We have made a virtue of people being 'free' to do their own thing. But, as John Stuart Mill pointed out, personal freedom is only real freedom so long as it doesn't inhibit the freedom of others.

The churches themselves have been affected by this cultural change, even if they are reluctant to admit it. It is evident in the fragmentation caused as new social and scientific ideas challenge old assumptions about, for example, the role of women, sexuality, the nature of the universe, and the supernatural. There is a growth of new sects, and some of the traditional church groupings are under threat from falling numbers. In such a climate symbols of unifying authority have less and less meaning, hence the decline in respect for the monarchy, parliament, and the Church.

So how is the Church responding to this culture shift? The most obvious reaction has been self-defence, manifested in greater conservatism. When under threat it is natural to barricade yourself in against the enemy, and to claim even more vehemently that your great truths were right all along, and in 'precisely the terms you chose to put them'. Accept them at face value or you are out. This is obviously a formula for exclusivism. More people are excluded from the churches than ever before, as theology is privatized by the very people who say they want to reach out in 'mission' to the population at large.

This analysis is supported by recent research carried out in East Anglia which showed a majority of Anglican churches in the sample to be exclusivist, taking a 'them' and 'us' attitude towards the community at large, and being reluctant to baptize the babies of those who do not attend church. The churches were so clublike, that the question had to be asked whether those called to the ordained ministry needed the skills of club officials and administrators, more than the skills required for public ministry, relating the Christian faith to all levels of society. In such an environment, those at the edge of faith, and those without the right vocabulary, wouldn't stand much of a chance.

An alternative response is 'inclusive', and more risky. It begins by accepting that the culture shift has happened, and is still in rapid motion; it sees that much of the criticism of old values is valid; it recognizes that Christ is always resourceful enough to be capable of being expressed in new ways consonant with the post-modern culture, so long as his story is read imaginatively alongside the new images and symbols that are being thrown up.

If Christianity does not take this second route, how is it to make any sense to those at the edge, and, just as importantly, how are those at the centre ever to discover the liberation of walking to the edge and finding there a whole new range of possibilities in God's repertoire? Theology has to avoid the bunker mentality at all costs, or it will become stale and increasingly isolated in a society that will be indifferent to its fate.

When Jesus spoke of insiders and outsiders he used the image of the Good Shepherd. The Good Shepherd tries to keep his fold secure and safe from predators, but he will go out into the wilderness to find a lost sheep, and will even lay down his life for his sheep. But in case the sheep of the fold should become complacent, they are reminded that there are other sheep not of this fold, for whom just as much effort will be made. The aim is that there should be one fold and one shepherd (John 10.1–18). It is as if Christ found his spiritual energy at the edge, saving the lost sheep, just as the Prodigal Son found spiritual renewal in a far country.

So the message to the churches, to dioceses, to synods, to seminaries, to all the introspective 'churchy' sects and subsects of Christianity is: there are other sheep I have who are not of this fold! The edge may be dangerous, but it is your duty to go out there and face it. Dare to walk over the edges of mundane human experience, and a new world will be opened.

Jesus on the Edge

All the gospel evidence suggests that Jesus lived at the edge of religious life too, not respecting the sacred cows of his religious contemporaries – strict sabbath day observance, ritual cleanliness, the religious isolation of women, the politics of the Temple – and that that was why he was crucified. They wouldn't have crucified an insider now, would they; neither would they have simply been actors in the divine epic of salvation, plotting Jesus' death because the script demanded it, like some karaoke song. They crucified Jesus because he dared to criticize and question; he was treading a forbidden path along the dangerous edge of their religious life.

What is more, Jesus himself, God incarnate, experiences the dangerous edge; literally so when he stands on the pinnacle of the Temple and is tempted to win converts by jumping off and surviving; also in the wilderness experience generally, and when he stood on a high mountain looking wistfully at the temporal power represented by 'all the kingdoms of the world'. This was the narrow boundary between loyalty and disloyalty, between fidelity and infidelity to God the Father.

Again in Gethsemane, Jesus stood at the edge when he prayed to his Father 'take this cup from me', and on the cross when he uttered the most haunting cry of history, 'My God, my God, why hast thou forsaken me?'

There are many other stories which show that Jesus accepted uncertainty as an entirely natural part of the religious quest: the father of the epileptic boy (Mark 9.14–29), who so movingly sought healing for his son, and was told that all things are possible to him who believes. He could have lied his way through – yes, Lord, I have complete confidence in your ability – but he was honest enough to say, 'Lord, I believe, help thou mine unbelief.'

Or Peter striding out over the water (Matthew 14.28–32)

to meet Jesus, when doubt overcomes him, and he sinks, and Jesus stretches out his hand to save him, saying, 'O Man of little faith; why did you doubt?'

But, while the dangerous edge is accepted as a natural part of the religious journey, on other occasions faith is presented as an essential prerequisite of receiving Christ's blessing. When Jesus cured two blind men (Matthew 9.27ff) their cure seemed conditional on their faith: 'Do you believe that I am able to do this?' he asks, and then adds, 'According to your faith be it done to you'. To Martha, before Lazarus' resurrection, Jesus says that whoever believes in him will have life, and Martha makes the same declaration which Peter made at Caesarea Philippi, which is the central acclamation of the gospels, 'Yes, Lord, I believe that you are the Christ'. And, of course, there is Jesus' response to 'Doubting' Thomas, 'Blessed are those who have not seen and yet believe'.

Thus, reading the gospels it is hard not to conclude that unwavering faith – the kind that can move mountains – is the ideal of Christian discipleship, yet reassuringly it is a goal that even the disciples themselves do not achieve: Thomas, Peter, Judas, and, presumably, James and John with their gauche request to sit at Christ's right and left hand in the kingdom of heaven.

I don't mean to make a virtue out of maverick behaviour; besides, if everyone didn't conform, you would simply have a new orthodoxy. I am more concerned that no one should think that they can see all there is to see from the point at which they are standing. One of the reasons for travel is to discover new culture, new ideas, new images, new colours, new tastes; and the experience can subsequently intensify the way you appreciate your familiar surroundings. So those who would *see* God must be willing to journey into the unexpected territories of faith, and not be complacent enough to say, no thanks I've got quite enough already. This means pilgrimage, which is what we do next, hopefully with some colourful postcards on the way.

CHAPTER 7

WALKING WITH GOD

> Noah was a righteous man, blameless in his generation; Noah walked with God.
>
> Genesis 6.9

> And we most humbly beseech thee, O heavenly Father, so to assist us with thy grace, that we may continue in that holy fellowship, and do all such works as thou hast prepared for us to walk in.
>
> The Book of Common Prayer

A Postcard from the Desert

George Steiner compares the human condition to Holy Saturday, poised between the despair of Good Friday on the one hand and the joy of Easter on the other. 'Ours is the long day's journey of the Saturday,' he says, 'between suffering, aloneness, unutterable waste on the one hand and the dream of liberation, of rebirth on the other'.[1] It is a metaphor of exodus and pilgrimage immediately recognizable to the Judaeo/Christian tradition in the stories of the Old Testament Patriarchs, and the life of Jesus who in St John's Gospel describes himself as the way, the truth, and the life.

In the Old Testament the wilderness years of the Exodus provide a great paradigm for the Jewish religious life – walking with God. This was the momentous journey from slavery to nationhood. But the journey itself was a time of testing, from the moment they left Egypt running before a pursuing army, to the subsequent ordeals of hunger, thirst, and disillusionment in the desert, almost ending in mutiny against Moses, and certainly making people wonder whether their faith in Yahweh was actually worth it. But this walk was *with God* who provided the miraculous heavenly manna and the spring of water struck from the rock.

Eventually the Jews came to reverence the nomadic experience as the groundwork of their faith. Thus in Deuteronomy, at the end of the chapter which contains the Ten Commandments, the people are told, 'You shall walk in all the way which the Lord your God commanded you, that you may live, and that it may go well with you, and that you may live long in the land which you shall possess' (Deuteronomy 5.33). The Hebrew word for 'walking in the way of the Lord', *halakah*, became the name given to the oral commentary on the written laws of Sinai. It is as if the text is the tradition, and the Jewish life is a commentary around it. As Psalm 1.1–2 puts it,

> Blessed is the man who walks not in the way of sinners,
> nor sits in the seat of scoffers; but his delight is in the
> law of the Lord, and on his law he meditates day and
> night.

(In later Judaism the *Halakah* was written down and applied to even the most trivial details of everyday life, resulting in the petty legalism criticized by Jesus in the gospels: for instance, plucking heads of grain on the sabbath day – Mark 12.23ff.)

Later in Deuteronomy the Israelite settler in the Promised Land is instructed always to remember his origins. The farmer must bring the first-fruits of his crop to the priest at the sanctuary and recite the words: 'My ancestor was a wandering Aramaean, a homeless refugee . . .' (Deuteronomy 26.5 GNB). He must undertake this ritual because his ancestors were wanderers, and he must remember that God delivered them out of Egypt and brought them to the Promised Land. But the ritual act of commemoration also reminds them of the moral and religious achievement of their nomadic ancestors. Amongst these virtues was the moral and physical discipline required to sustain a close-knit, tent-dwelling society. They must be united against the predation of man and beast, even-handed in common ownership, intensely loyal in religious, tribal, and sexual relationship. They had little time for ritual and never stayed anywhere long enough to get entangled with the local religions. It is the respect of God and neighbour, and the nostalgically remembered simple life of the wilderness tribes, that is held up as a model in the spiritual heritage of later Israel.

At the time of the monarchy, when corruption in national life reached its height, the protesting voices of Elijah and Amos, who spoke for Yahweh, were voices which came 'from the wilderness'. Indeed the basic moral code, the Ten Commandments, which shaped Israelite religion so decisively, was established in the wilderness, in the walking years.

It doesn't take much to see how this great theme is reflected in the Christian story. The infant Christ is visited by shepherds, the inheritors of the nomadic, pastoral tradition. John the Baptist, the great prophet of the messianic age, emerges from the wilderness dressed in a coat of camel's hair, and Jesus himself wanders into the wilderness as a means of spiritual preparation and cleansing for the ministry he is about to undertake. 'My ancestor was a wandering Aramaean, a homeless refugee'. As Jesus said himself, 'Foxes have holes and birds of the air have nests, but the Son of Man hath nowhere to lay his head.' And at the end of the story, Jesus was crucified outside the city of Jerusalem, symbolically back in the wilderness.

Not only is the Son of Man a wandering prophet, but he is in a mystical sense himself the path of life – the way, the truth, and the life – through whom men and women can come to God, so long as they are prepared to tread the same road by which he himself goes to God, the *Via Dolorosa*, the way of the cross, which is proclaimed in the gospel preaching, 'If any man would come after me, let him deny himself and take up his cross and follow me' (Mark 8.34). This image is so strong that in the early Church Christ's religion was known as 'the Way'. Thus Paul persecutes those belonging to the Way (Acts 9.2) and proudly admits in his defence before Felix that he worships 'according to the Way, which they call a sect' (Acts 24.14).

Over the centuries Christian pilgrims have symbolized their commitment to follow Christ's way by undertaking journeys to holy places as a means of spiritual renewal. Many who have visited Jerusalem have retraced the path of the *Via Dolorosa*, sometimes carrying a cross themselves; and in the seventeenth century it was possible for a pilgrim to Jerusalem to have tattooed on his wrists a cross surrounded by the words *Via, Veritas, Vita*.[2]

A Postcard from Down Under

In his novel about spiritual journeying, *The Song Lines*, Bruce Chatwin describes his travels around Australian aboriginal settlements in search of information about the indigenous religion. The song lines are ancient tracks made of songs which tell of the creation of the land. As the nomadic aboriginals travel, their ritual is to sing the songs of their ancestors, which function partly as a kind of map, and partly as a means of creating the world afresh. It is not surprising that a nomadic people should see life as a 'walk'.

Half-way through the book, he breaks away from traditional narrative novel-writing and produces nearly a hundred pages of 'notes'. These notes are a medley of quotations, parables, epigrams, strange facts, and short stories, skilfully woven together, rather like a gospel. He uses this section as a commentary, or *halakah*, on the novel he is in the process of writing. It is a kind of prodding of the reader to recognize the concepts that underpin his travelogue. In that sense it is like the relation of doctrine to the Bible – the distillation of the ideas expanded in the story-telling parts of the text.

The theme is the contrast between exploration and settlement. Chatwin investigates man's restlessness and wanderlust, and talks about the primitive suspicion of cities as places of violence and corruption. In a typical 'note', he writes: 'Jahweh, in origin, is a God of the Way. His sanctuary is the mobile Ark, his house a tent, his Altar a cairn of rough stones. And though He may *promise* His Children a well-watered land ... he secretly desires for them the Desert.'[3]

The book of Exodus instructs that the Passover must be eaten with 'sandals on your feet, and your staff in your hand; and you shall eat it in haste' (Exodus 12.11). This reminds the Jews that their vitality lies in movement. When Jesus sent his disciples out on a mission, he told them to 'take nothing for their journey except a staff ... but to wear sandals' (Mark 6.8–9). The medieval pilgrim had this text in mind when he carried a staff as a symbol of his spiritual journey, reminding him that Christianity's vitality lies in movement too.

Chatwin obviously prefers exploration to settlement. But the interdependence of the two is undeniable. In Afghanistan, at harvest time, he notes, nomads and farmers are the best of friends: the nomads buy grain for winter. 'The villagers buy cheese, hides, and meat. They welcome the sheep on their fields to break up the stubble, and manure it for the autumn planting.'[4]

Which, then, is the more appropriate image for the Christian, nomad or settler, searcher or the one who has found? Perhaps we need both perspectives, just as we need to experience God as divine other and personal presence. God's 'transcendence' needs to be searched out by travelling, but God's 'immanence' is already found. This is what Pascal must have meant when he said of God, 'You would not be seeking me if you had not already found me'.

And here's an interesting twist. The nomads can in fact stop long enough at a fertile spot to cultivate and harvest a crop of corn, but they can never make wine because a vine takes years to establish before it is ready to produce suitable grapes. This gives a new dimension to the symbols of bread and wine at the eucharist: bread of the nomads, wine of the settlers; bread reminiscent of the manna in the wilderness, and wine reminiscent of Cana and Pentecost.

The word 'travel', as we are often reminded, comes from the same root as 'travail' – toil, exertion, hardship, even, in biblical language, the pangs of childbirth – a woman in travail. The medieval pilgrims, whose journeys, especially to Compostela and Jerusalem, were horribly hard and dangerous, combined into a single ritual the Old Testament walk with God and the wilderness experience. They considered *walking* the most spiritually improving method of travel because it is more demanding than riding on a horse, but also perhaps because it provides the right rhythm and pace for reflection. I can see their point; jetting to a destination is scarcely to travel at all, certainly not to travail, despite what people might say about air-traffic controllers. The boredom of airport lounges and in-flight entertainment is tiresome precisely because it is *not* travail, not active. But to walk (or even to drive – on the minor roads) through gradually changing terrain and climatic conditions, gives a sense of scale, history, distance.

It's ironic that in this age of mass tourism, when travel is no longer the prerogative of a wealthy élite, but easily available to millions, that the metaphor of journeying for spiritual discovery should need to be argued for. On second thoughts it's not such a surprise, because I suppose the 'Slough of Despond', 'The Valley of Humiliation', 'Vanity Fair', and the 'Doubting Castle' of Bunyan's *Pilgrim's Progress* are simply bypassed on the motorway.

So let me see if I can dig out from my grandmother's drawer a postcard or two from the ancient nomadic journeying texts of the past. What would we expect to find? I think they will highlight the dangers of journeys, and reveal the complexity and ambiguity of encounters made on the way.

From the Land of Moriah

The biblical travelogue begins with Abraham (known at this point as Abram, prior to the covenant with God). God says to Abram, 'Go from your country and your kindred and your father's house to the land which I will show you' (Genesis 12.1). It was a big move, but Abram had nothing to lose and everything to gain, so he went. The Epistle to the Hebrews sees this as a model of faith, 'By faith Abraham obeyed ... and went out not knowing where he was to go' (Hebrews 11.8). The question Hebrews is trying to answer is: if salvation comes through faith in Jesus Christ, what happened to those who lived before Christ? Well, they could be saved by faith if they had recognized Christ's promises 'from afar', because 'faith is the assurance of things hoped for', things journeyed towards. Thus, Hebrews builds up an elaborate image of life as a pilgrimage. We are strangers and exiles on the earth who desire a better country, a heavenly city, a new Jerusalem (11.13-16), and the Christian life is like the Exodus of the Old Testament, moving from enslavement to the Promised Land, with the long day's journey of the Saturday in between.

Abram travelled. He went to Egypt to escape famine, and saved himself by allowing his wife to become Pharaoh's mistress. He left a rich man, along with Lot, also wealthy. The two parted company, Lot taking the Jordan Valley, and Abraham heading off to the west, ending up at Hebron, south of Jerusalem.

But Abraham's most famous journey must surely be the one when he sets out for Mount Moriah to sacrifice Isaac. Let me just remind you of the background. Sarah was infertile; Abraham was getting old. A childless woman in that culture was nothing, and she had had to bear the humiliation of allowing her maid servant, Hagar, to bear Abraham a son who they called Ishmael. Then God promised that they would have a child of their own. Everyone laughed including Sarah, but this was to be a 'child of promise' on whom the future of the nation depended. How absurd, therefore, that God should demand his ritual murder, and how absurd for Abraham cold-bloodedly to agree without so much as a protest. Ah, but Abraham had faith; he knew that God would provide – and events proved him right. Possibly true, but too simplistic, and fails to do justice to this complex text which bristles with ambiguity about our relationship to God.

I once wrote a children's play about this, but the mothers protested so much about the cruelty of the plot that it was never performed. They decided this bit of scripture was a scandal and they ruled it out of court. They knew the utter moral outrage that Sarah would have felt, had she known what was going on. No child must ever think that a parent could do such a thing. 'Here, Father, are the fire and the wood, but where is the young beast for the sacrifice?' This surely, of all moments in scripture, was the moment for apostasy, the moment to abandon the tyrant God and espouse atheism. If Abraham had any moral backbone he would have challenged God, and damned the consequences.

Yet Abraham is praised for his absolute obedience to God, the mark of a religious man. But such piety cannot stem the tide of questioning: why does the text not challenge the notion of human sacrifice? Why, when Isaac realizes that *he* is the sacrifice, does Abraham remain unmoved? Is Abraham unruffled because he believes that God can raise people from the dead, and therefore Isaac will be raised again? This is certainly the view of the Epistle to the Hebrews (11.19). Really! Or should the emphasis be on *Isaac*? Is he an icon for Christ as the Lamb of God? Irenaeus says that the devout should take up their cross as Isaac took up his bundle of sticks. For Abraham, and for us, this is a journey into the dark night of the soul, and into the nature of God.

POSTCARDS ON THE WAY TO HEAVEN

Crossing the Pyrenees

I was thinking about Abraham and Isaac when I first read a poem by John Matthias, which seemed to me a brilliant, if unintended, commentary on the story. I hope it will not be considered an insult if I use this as my 'postcard' from the Pyrenees, because I consider this one of the most colourful and moving statements there could be from the road to heaven. It speaks of a pilgrimage to Santiago de Compostela in Northern Spain, where the remains of St James the Apostle are thought to rest. In the Middle Ages it was the most important place of Christian pilgrimage after Jerusalem and Rome. The overland routes were dotted with guest-houses.

Dedication to a Cycle of Poems on the Pilgrim Routes to Santiago de Compostela – John Matthias

This is for my daughter, who
in the middle of the map I try to draw, this making,
struggles to a Compostela of her own
in pain & torment. *What did I do wrong?* she asks.
What did I do wrong
to suffer this? – The primal, secret, terrified & universal

query of the sick. She did nothing wrong.
And yet she walks in chains
along a Lemosina or a Tolosona Dolorosa

winding through uncertainty and grief
to disappear into unknowable remote far distances.
She walks ahead of me, doubting that

I follow, although I call out loudly & I try.
But also, when she herself must rest, unable to go on,
at hospital or hospice on the way, then

WALKING WITH GOD

I'll learn to wait, a patient too, without impatience.
Perhaps we'll see pass by every single other living soul!
The routes were arduous, each one,

and cemeteries in the churchyards far outnumber
monuments recording cures miraculous
achieved along the way. You had to get there somehow.

You had to show the saint your poor
tormented frail human body. You had to drag it there
driven by your guilt or your desire.

The journey's so entirely strange I cannot fathom it.
And yet this map, this prayer:
That she will somehow get to Compostela,

take that how you may, & that I will be allowed to
follow.
And that Santiago, call him what you like,
Son of Thunder, Good Saint Jacques, The Fisherman,

or whoever really lies there –
hermit, heretic, shaman healer with no name –
will somehow make us whole.

Here is a father, in some sense like Abraham, making a pilgrimage, but to the Spanish shrine of Santiago de Compostela, rather than to Mount Moriah. In his mind he takes with him his cancer-stricken daughter. Or is she taking him? – 'She walks ahead of me, doubting that I follow.'

In this pilgrimage, like all serious pilgrimages, the outer journey is a metaphor for the inner journey of the spirit. But what does the spirit seek? Healing? An explanation for why there is suffering, 'the primal, secret, terrified & universal query of the sick'? Patience? The divine Other, represented by 'whoever really lies there' in this shrine, traditionally associated with St James the Apostle?

All of these and more, no doubt. The father's journey has become a metaphor for life itself — a journey 'so entirely strange I cannot fathom it', he says. Yet his daughter who 'struggles to a Compostela of her own in pain & torment', and rests 'at hospital or hospice on the way', seems to have the journey better fathomed. She seems to have found a resilience and inner strength which can only move her father, and make him feel impotent beside her struggle. So he is drawing a map — and this is to me the most striking image of the poem — he is drawing a map for her and for him, and presumably for those who will follow after into this unknown, yet all too familiar, territory. And this map is his prayer 'that she will somehow get to Compostela, take that how you may' — Mount Moriah, Peniel, Golgotha, Emmaus, heaven, healing, God — who 'will somehow make us whole'.

Isaac is not, of course, a physically sick child as is this girl, and Abraham's almost fundamentalist religious clumsiness is in stark contrast to the sensitive heart-searching of her father, yet all four characters are caught up in the ambiguity, and sometimes seemingly insuperable obstacles which impede the road to heaven. In Genesis, Abraham and Isaac actually reach Moriah and there are confronted by 'the primal, secret, terrified & universal query'; in his poem, Matthias never actually reaches Santiago, but is always *en route*. He says in his notes to *A Gathering of Ways*,

> The writing became a pilgrimage in earnest when, without warning, I had first to help another person struggle towards physical and spiritual health, and then, unwell myself, begin a similar journey of my own.

The Wrestlers

Jacob, of course, was the grandson of Abraham, and to

understand the story we need to take a glance at Jacob's *curriculum vitae*. He's the son of Isaac and Rebekah, twin brother of Esau, the red and hairy one, who was born first, with Jacob clutching on to his heel as if to say, 'Wait for me!'

If Esau was his daddy's boy, Jacob was mummy's pet. What would Freud have to say about this? In early manhood impetuous Esau is tricked out of his birthright by his brother for a bowl of lentil soup, with Rebekah, like Lady Macbeth, sweet-talking the lad into treachery.

Life began at forty for Esau when he married Judith, but for some undisclosed reason they didn't get on with the parents. Nevertheless when Isaac was nearly blind and thought he was about to die he decided to give his paternal blessing to his older son, Esau. But with Rebekah still plotting power for her favourite man, Jacob is egged on by his mother to give his famous hairy man impression of Esau. Rebekah even prepares the savoury game pie which charms the old man and seals the bid to cheat Esau of his rightful blessing. Surprise, surprise, Esau did not like Jacob and was hell-bent on revenge.

So Jacob made a judicious career move and went to Mesopotamia, to Paddan-aram to court the daughters of his uncle Laban.

When he reached Bethel Jacob had his famous ladder dream, in which God promised him and his descendants a sort of freehold on the land which he was leaving. It was a numinous experience about which he said afterwards, 'How awesome is this place! This is none other than the house of God, and this is the gate of heaven' (Genesis 28.17).

In Haran, Jacob contracted to Laban to work for seven years in return for the hand of his beautiful daughter, Rachel. On the wedding night Laban substituted his heavily veiled elderly ugly daughter, Leah, on the grounds that it was not the custom to let the younger daughter marry first. Jacob was not amused, but could scarcely complain – had he not cheated his own father by dressing up in his brother's clothes?

A week later Jacob married Rachel but had to pay off Laban

with another seven years work. With this harem of Leah, Rachel and their maids Zilpah and Bilhah, Jacob set about the momentous business of fathering the twelve tribes of Israel:

> to Leah six sons: Reuben, Simeon, Levi and Judah. Subsequently: Issachar and Zebulun, and a daughter, Dinah
> to Bilhah two sons: Dan and Naphtali
> to Zilpah two sons: Gad and Asher
> to Rachel two sons: Joseph, and Benjamin (very much an afterthought. Rachel died in childbirth.)

Jacob got his own back on Laban by swindling him out of a fortune in livestock, and departed from Haran a wealthy man; but the prospect of returning home is filled with the monstrous spectre of Esau, his cheated brother, whom he must meet again face to face. Jacob is a prodigal returning from a far country, not to a father but to a brother! And you remember the attitude of the older brother in Jesus' parable. Jacob cannot hope to be accepted, such was the treachery of his behaviour twenty years before, and this crippling anxiety brings on not so much a mid-life crisis as a spiritual breakdown.

What happened that dreadful night in Genesis chapter 32 by the Ford of Jabbok? Having sent his wives, their maids, his children, and all his worldly goods across the river, Jacob stood completely alone, disinherited, just as Esau had been twenty years before. He remembered what it was like to be a wandering refugee stripped of his identity and his possessions. But he was not alone; the spectre of his cheated brother haunted him in every shadow.

The darkness and solitude played tricks with his mind and he began to feel a frightening presence, so that he said to himself, 'If I stay here I will die'. He decided to set off immediately for the tents of his family, but as he crossed the river he was resisted by a silent figure who emerged from the darkness. The resistance turned to coarse wrestling with no holds barred, no conventions observed, each man for himself. This was Jacob's style. The mysterious force grabbed Jacob between the legs and dislocated his thigh with a ripping tear which left him lame. But Jacob held on with the same tenacity as he had held on to his brother's heel at birth. And as he struggled he had the weird sensation that he was fighting God, and some of God's strength was being transferred to him. Why should God, his guardian, become his opponent? It was an unnerving thought, like betrayal. But incredibly Jacob seemed to be winning, holding God down until he begs to be released. He was standing up to God, with all the effrontery that Abraham ought to have shown in the land of Moriah. This was his nature, the reckless chancer with an inflated sense of his own destiny. 'I will not let you go unless you bless me', he says to God. But God is not as gullible as blind old Isaac, and he disarms Jacob by demanding to know his name. To know a man's name was to know a man's nature, and Jacob's bubble is pricked as he has to admit that his name means 'cheat'. God says that that will not do as a name for his people, so he gives him a new name, and a new nature, the name of 'Israel', by which the Jewish people have been known across the centuries.

'And tell me your name,' he says to his assailant, but you don't ask God his name. Moses tried and was told, 'I am that I am'. You wrestle with your intellect to know the name of the divine Other, but there is no answer, no name, and yet, paradoxically, in the painful process you have actually encountered the divine mystery. It is this disclosure of the transcendence of God that is Jacob's blessing. Thus Jacob/Israel goes away from the Jabbok blessed, but limping.

And what we have seen in this short episode, sandwiched between the much longer passages describing Jacob in Haran and the Joseph narratives, is the heart of the religious quest, the long day's journey of the Saturday, man clutching at God for his power of blessing. It illustrates with intense dramatic power the experience of searching for our moral and religious self, and in the grip of God's power, wrestling for selfhood, identity and meaning.

But it is a *fight*, and the blessing is *ambiguous*. On this night, when Jacob became Israel, he sustained a crippling injury, and in a sense he goes away from God a broken man, limping. Being chosen by God also means being crippled by him. This may seem surprising in view of the messianic prophecy, 'Then shall the lame man leap like a hart' (Isaiah 35.6), but it remains the most telling truth revealed on the road to heaven. The great Old Testament scholar, Gerhard von Rad, says that in this story, 'Israel has here presented its entire history with God almost prophetically as such a struggle until the break of day',[5] and so it is for the Christian pilgrim.

I suppose some might argue that I am understating the good news of healing and resurrection, and overstating a personal fondness for 'wrestling Jacob'. But I'm particularly anxious that people should acknowledge the *cost* of discipleship, and not fall for an easy, triumphalist Christianity that loses its shine as soon as some personal setback or suffering gets in the way. The pattern of infatuation followed by disillusionment is seen too often in the modern Church, and reminds me of the seeds which fell on shallow soil and sprang up quickly, but were soon scorched by the sun, and died because they had no roots (Matthew 13.5–7). Naturally, I wish to proclaim the new life which Christ brings, but it is a life in which you cannot walk confidently and joyfully until first you have limped. Even Christ himself, who was in perfect harmony with God, was lamed on the cross before he walked the Road to Emmaus.

If the image of a journey into the life of God is a good model for Christian discipleship, then it implies all the changing fortunes of a journey, too – changeable weather, beautiful mountains one day, monotonous lowland the next, illness in a country where you can't speak the language, unbearable humidity, insects ... Similarly, Christian discipleship offers the sunshine of spiritual wholeness, but doesn't protect a person from pain – either physical or spiritual. God helps people to cope with pain, disease, and disappointment, but he doesn't remove it.

Postcards from the New World

So far my examples have been overtly religious. Every now and then I get a brochure through the post from some travel company or other trying to sell special-interest holidays to holy places. They usually begin (as do letters from funeral directors) 'Reverend and esteemed Sir', and promise a spiritual experience in the footsteps of St Paul, and a free passage if I find ten others to go with me. But religious holidays, like religious drama, or cathedral coffee shops, never sound as exciting as the real thing. Besides, if God is found not only in *holy* scripture, it is pretty likely that God will not be found only in holy places either. All places have the potential to be hallowed ground. All journeys have the potential to expand our relationship with God, but particularly those driven by the pioneering spirit into new territory, and new opportunity. The modern travel industry is a residual organ, an appendix, of this deep-seated human instinct. Ask any beauty queen or lottery ticket buyer what they most hope for, and more than likely they'll reply, 'Well, I'd like to travel'. The wanderlust runs deep.

When I visited the Immigration Hall on Ellis Island in New York harbour, I found its power to expand the image repertoire palpable. This was the building through which millions of immigrants came into the United States, desperate to escape poverty in Europe, or, if they were Jews, the pogroms of the Jewish ghettoes. They crossed the Atlantic packed in ships like cattle, in a voyage that would last four or five weeks. Many never discovered where the toilets were.

The vast and bleak Hall, inhuman in scale, is now a

museum. The hundreds of sensitively displayed photographs reveal the people who once inhabited it – dishevelled characters waiting in pens with their bundles of ragged clothes and battered suitcases, staring sheepishly at officials who had the power to admit them to the 'Land of the Free', or send them back on the next ship. Here they were deloused and checked for infectious disease, blindness and handicap. The sick were sorted from the fit like victims in a concentration camp. A man might be separated from his wife, a mother from her children, a single child from its family, to be sent home. Those who were fit had to decide between family loyalty and a future – between despair and despair. Some individuals about whom the authorities were uncertain would be kept overnight, sleeping in dormitories in canvas bunks, four deep and twelve wide, slung across the room in a metal frame, like drawers in a filing cabinet, people in the pending tray of life and death. Some had jumped into the harbour waters and drowned rather than make the wretched and hopeless journey back across the ocean.

The tenacity of the human spirit in search of new life and in escape from economic hardship and persecution is awesome. A woman in the fast-food restaurant told me she had come through these buildings as a babe in arms. She had looked at the exhibition half-wondering whether she might see a picture of herself. As she relived in her imagination the ordeal her parents must have endured she felt physically sick, and guilty that perhaps they had suffered this indignity on her behalf. Now for her, and thousands of other visiting Americans, the pilgrimage to Ellis Island is a solemn re-enactment of the struggle of their forebears, a sacrament of the spirit that enabled them to bear such deprivation in the search for a new life and new values. 'My ancestor was a wandering Aramaean, a homeless refugee'. It is a holy thing to remember the hardship of your ancestors.

A week later I visited the Museum of Air and Space in Washington DC. Suspended in the vast entrance foyer is a small single-prop aeroplane, the legendary 'Spirit of St Louis', flown by Lindbergh in 1927 on the first solo flight across the Atlantic. He took 33 hours at a speed of little over one hundred miles an hour, in this diminutive and antique machine.

At the other end of the hall is the spidery moon-landing craft, seemingly fragile, and absurdly wrapped, like a toffee, in silver and gold foil to protect it from dangerous rays, and the impact of meteoric micro-dust. I thought I wouldn't let my daughter go to school in it, let alone to the moon. Yet men had endured monumental journeys in both these craft, in cramped conditions less spacious than those afforded to the immigrants, in search of new horizons, and risking their lives to achieve what no one had ever done before.

What was so noble about all this? Where was the spiritual meaning? Weren't the whole lot of them doing it for themselves? Amerigo Vespucci, Columbus, da Gama, Captain Cook were all seeking fame and fortune. Those who went to the moon were in one sense fighting the Cold War, proving to Russia that America possessed a technology which spelled the words, 'Watch out'. But they were also searching for a new world, a new order. One of the astronauts, so overwhelmed with the eerie presence of God, became a fervent evangelical Christian. Yet you might say that all this pioneering was a far cry from the humble walk with God. The immigrants believed that the streets of the new world were paved with gold, and the Apollo missions were a celebration of material success. Were they not all trying to gain the whole world? And we remember what Jesus said about that.

And yet, their spirit of exploration, that urge and drive to reach out into the unknown, is surely the same psychological force that impels men and women to explore their religious faith as a means of finding a new life of fulfilment. As Paul says, 'When anyone is united to Christ, there is a new world; the old order has gone' (2 Corinthians 5.17 NEB). The journey is all a great parable of our imperfection and our reaching out for God.

Home, Sweet Home

My mother hated holidays, and the furthest she ever went was to Dieppe on a day trip from Newhaven. She much preferred to stay at home where she felt safe, and where it didn't cost so much money. 'We've got plenty of beautiful countryside on our doorstep,' she said, which of course was true. She would have been in agreement with Martin Luther who criticized pilgrims for neglecting both Christ and their neighbours at home, 'in order to spend ten times as much money away from home without having any results and merit to show for it'.[6] Luther's argument was, of course, directed against the granting of indulgences to those who made pilgrimages to Jerusalem and Rome, but he clearly thought travel a bit of an indulgence in itself.

See you in Prague.

CHAPTER 8

A PILGRIMAGE TO PRAGUE

> Remembering and hoping are the dynamic forces moving the pilgrim along his way, a way through the wilderness filled with threats and danger.[1]
>
> John Navone

In December 1990 I attended the Taizé European Meeting in Prague with a group from the University Church 'Taizé Prayer' congregation. They were all students, except for my curate, Michael Roden, Caroline Higginbottom, and her daughter Kate, who was then fifteen.

The ecumenical Taizé Community, founded by Brother Roger, in the village of that name in Burgundy, France, near Cluny, is a place of pilgrimage for young people, where they can meet for discussion and worship. The style of the worship is characterized by the repetitive singing of chants in four-part harmony. Each winter, between Christmas and New Year, the community holds a meeting in one of the great European cities, and recreates its worship and ethos in churches and school halls.

This postcard from Prague is one of those that concertinas out to show different pictures of the city, and provides space for a lot of writing!

View over the Rooftops

I suppose I ought to admit now that I had gone to see *Prague*, not to sit about in a tent all day singing religious ditties in Latin, French or Polish, with a load of kids. Prague conjured up Kafka's Castle, *Good King Wenceslas*, the 'Prague Spring',

Don Giovanni, and Milan Kundera's *Book of Laughter and Forgetting*. I had been told that it was the most beautiful city in Europe, and I wanted to see it for myself.

From the religious point of view, my presence there wasn't totally fraudulent, however. I can take Taizé worship in small doses, and I was keen to find out what had kept religion going under communist repression, when even the priests had been controlled by state licence. I think all of us were in a curious way jealous of the spiritual energy which repression and exile generates, and wanted to capture some of this energy for ourselves, and take it away in a bottle like Jordan water.

Eighty thousand people piled into Prague – equivalent to an increase of ten per cent in the city's population. For four days the trams and underground trains were packed with rucksacked youths in walking-boots with oatmeal socks rolled over the top. Many came from other parts of Eastern Europe – Poland, Rumania, Hungary. They slept on school floors and wherever space could be found, and were fed by the Czech army, with Russian army surplus tins of hot beef and spaghetti, in the open air outside massive tents on the Letna Plain, which had been erected to house the twice-daily prayers. These were the size of football pitches, and thousands gathered inside sitting on the ground in the lotus position, grouped by nationality, to pray in the simple and familiar chants of Taizé.

St Ignatius' Church

At 3.30 pm each afternoon during the Meeting the English and the Russians met in the faded baroque church of St Ignatius to listen to a meditation given by one of the Taizé brothers. These talks were translated sentence by sentence into Russian with the consequence that the speaker had to think in sentences rather than paragraphs, presenting us with a series of pensées. Sometimes (as in the case of Pope John Paul II) the broken English accent added weight to a familiar point. 'I understand that in Engleesh the word "heal" also means "to make whole". God accepts the whole of you, as you are.'

That's great. It's nice to feel internal reconciliation between you and God, but in this context there were big issues still waiting to be reconciled: years of the Cold War, the Russian emasculation of Czechoslovakia, rifts going back to 1939, Czechs and Slavs, historic racial tensions throughout Eastern Europe smouldering away under the joyful façade of liberation. But I felt much of the talk was directed towards a personal, contemporary consolation. It needed to be matched with judgement and challenge. God accepts you, but at the same time he has expectations of you. He accepts you as the person he created, but he does not necessarily accept the lifestyle you have chosen or the deeds you have done. Just as the first thrust of Jesus' ministry was the call to repentance, so repentance is the first challenge of God's acceptance. Only now as I write this does it occur to me that not once in the whole of this European Meeting was there a corporate act of penitence.

However, on our last afternoon in St Ignatius' Church there was a kind of redemption. At the end of the talks it had become customary to sing together, and on this occasion two small groups, one from Russia and one from the Ukraine, stood up to sing. The Ukrainians, in colourful national costume, sang old religious folk-songs, and the packed congregation, some sitting on the floor and many standing at the back, on tiptoe craning their necks to see, became completely silent, absorbed. Then the Russians sang – a group of five singers who intoned music of an unmistakably Orthodox flavour. The soprano possessed a beautifully melodious voice and the bass sang oily low notes that seemed impossible to reach. The music cried out to God, it stretched forth its hands, it came from the heart of oppressed people, and must have touched the heart of God. This was a moment of disclosure, and, to me, the most religious moment in a week of pilgrimage.

Somehow, the combination of music and an unexpected synergy of sounds, costumes, traditions, and live performance, had symbolized and expressed the very thing that the expenditure of many words had failed to do.

Old Town Square

On the fifth day Caroline, Kate, and I had decided to do some sightseeing in the Old Town Square. On the steps of St Nicholas' Church, a magnificent baroque Christmas cake next to the birthplace of Franz Kafka, we bumped into Boris. Boris was tall, opinionated and fine-boned, with the slight stoop of an intellectual. He taught Indian history in Moscow, but had never been allowed by the Russians to visit India because of his liberal political views. I had made his acquaintance after one of the soothing talks in St Ignatius'. At this present moment he looked bewildered, like a rat trapped in a maze.

He slipped quickly out of the church, and took my elbow with a glance to the right and to the left. I remembered how he had done exactly the same on the underground station, as if every conversation must be steered out of earshot.

'No, no. I don't need any coffee,' he said. 'But I will walk with you. Have you seen the Jewish Ghetto yet? I discovered it with a few of our chaps this morning.'

'Where *did* you learn your English, Boris?' I asked.

He seemed affronted.

'Why?' he asked.

'Where did you get all this "chaps" from – it's so absurdly idiomatic.'

'I studied at school in Moscow, of course. Where else? And I have read much of your literature. I learned to speak Italian by reading Dante's *Divine Comedy*, you know.'

I noticed later, in the street and on the tram going back to the flat, that whenever he heard English conversation, even amongst complete strangers, he butted in with some bright remark. He seemed to be posing as an Englishman abroad, partly for self-protection in a city that had good reason to dislike Russians, and partly because he was a Russian sick of Russia. His anorak and shoes were Western so it wasn't a difficult part to play. The only tell-tale signs that this was his first trip out of Russia was that he always clung on to a crinkled plastic bag containing food, and that every time he spoke he seemed to duck away from his interlocutor with a nervous stoop.

Josephtown

'The Jewish Cemetery is down this way. No, this street, I think. I am sorry, I don't have a map and my direction is not good.'

'Why do you want to go there again if you saw it this morning?' asked Kate.

'Because of my grandmother. My grandmother was a Jew. She once was in Bohemia.'

'Is she buried here?'

'I don't know where she is buried. She went to China, and then back to Russia. She was in a camp, you know.'

'She died in a camp?'

'Yes.'

'And your mother?'

'My mother? She escaped.'

The Cemetery is said to be one of the most interesting sights in Europe. It winds narrowly around an ancient synagogue and between high buildings, under the cover of trees which even in winter, when they have shed their leaves, cast a gloom over the underworld of stones. These stones, which all date prior to 1787, are rough-hewn and dense; they jut and slant, overcrowding one another like bad teeth in a crocodile. Bodies have been piled upon bodies so that the Cemetery has become a range of little hills with memorials planted wherever there is a space. It seems that this graveyard stands as a prophetic sign, in judgement of what was to come in the twentieth century, a sign of the seventy-seven thousand Jews from Bohemia and Moravia who were to die in the Holocaust.

Cafés and Pubs

By now the afternoon light was fading rapidly and our breath was suddenly visible in the night air. The others were hungry and wanted to eat. A nearby restaurant advertised a plate of goulash and dumplings for sixty crowns, just one pound sterling, and Kate pleaded with us to go in.

'Want to try the native cooking?' she asked Boris.

'No, I am not hungry, thank you,' he said.

'Well, we can either eat here or go back to the apartment for a snack,' I suggested.

'I would be very interested to see your apartment, if it's not an inconvenience to you,' said Boris.

As we walked towards the tram-stop in Narodni, I asked Boris how much money he had been able to bring. Any connection between this question and his reluctance to enter a coffee shop or restaurant was quite unconscious on my part. Through his nose he uttered an ironic 'Hah'. Then sniggered again and took me by the elbow.

'In Moscow the banks do not want crowns, and in Prague no one wants roubles,' he shrugged.

The implications of this statement shocked me, because with hard currency and a favourable exchange rate I had felt so ludicrously rich in this city. During this whole week Boris had not been able to buy a single Pilzen lager, not an orange to supplement the vitamin-deficient diet of the army food, nor a tiny memento of his first visit abroad. No wonder he clung on to the plastic bag which contained bread and cheese provided by Taizé for the long train journey back to Moscow. Kate whispered to me that I should buy him some fruit. When I gave it to him he protested and proudly gestured me away. 'No. I don't need it. I am very happy with what I have. I have enough.' My initial reaction was to feel I was patronizing him, and had stepped over some invisible line which marked the boundaries of dignity and friendship.

'Please,' I insisted with unaccustomed Latin demonstrativeness, almost embracing him, 'this is a gift of friendship, a gift of our days together in Prague.' And I pushed the fruit into his plastic bag.

Strasnice

Half an hour later we sat round the kitchen table of our third-floor apartment in the grey suburb of Strasnice, with the central heating blaring. Boris studiously observed my tea ritual, anxious to learn the art of tea-making from a genuine Englishman, and ate his way through a packet of 'Garibaldi' biscuits, which I had brought from home as emergency supplies. I explained these were known to most children as squashed fly biscuits, but Caroline informed him they were named after an Italian general whose men had been given such biscuits as rations.

'War,' she reflected wearily, 'always war and repression. War in the Gulf, Russian tanks ready to flatten the Baltic states. Even the biscuits remind us of war.'

'But we pray for reconciliation. We must always pray for reconciliation,' said Boris.

'What are we to believe?' she asked. 'What is God up to?'

'I'm sorry. I don't understand,' he said.

'I mean him,' she looked up and presumably beyond the browned ceiling and its sparsely shaded light bulb, 'he has a lot to answer for, don't you think?'

'Oh Mum, why blame God? What's it got to do with him?' laughed Kate, with the assured realism of a fifteen-year-old.

'He doesn't reconcile us, though, does he? Even Boris here will not take communion with a Catholic because the

Orthodox have the truth and the Catholics do not. What basis for reconciliation is that?'

Boris was not amused. One ought to have understood that the magnetism of the Cemetery in Josephstown and his insistence that we should make a pilgrimage with him there was an instinct, like the magnetic pull on a salmon back to its spawning ground. It was the second time he had been there that day, and, of all the corners of Prague he had discovered, he wanted us to see that. He was a Jewish convert to Orthodoxy, and possessed all the zealotry of a convert, while retaining a festering sense of guilt at having betrayed the suffering of his forefathers and foremothers, and Abraham, Isaac and Jacob and the rest.

'The truth is not won easily; just look around you,' he said, going to the open window which framed a picture of brown, smog-shrouded, communist tower blocks looming in the darkness. 'As far as your religion is concerned, I hope one day you will see it.' The Russian smiled.

I began to distrust Boris, because only two days before in the underground he had confided in me, with much suspicious glancing from side to side that in Moscow the Orthodox say the Holy Spirit of other denominations is the foot of the devil. He had said this as if their opinion were a blasphemy, and now he put them on the side of irrefutable truth.

'Where are you going now? I will come with you,' he said.

I explained that we would take the number 22 tram to I. P. Pavlova, and the metro from there to Vysehrad. At I. P. Pavlova the tram stops adjacent to the stairs down into the underground. All four of us got off, said short goodbyes as if we would all meet again in the morning, and Boris, clutching his plastic bag, disappeared into the night.

Three weeks later he sent me a Christmas card. It read,

> Due to the difference between Gregorian and Julian calendars I still can congratulate you with Christmas which we celebrate on the seventh of January.

> Wouldn't you agree now that the very traditionalism of our Church can sometimes do us good?
>
> Thank you very much for the fruits. There were so many of them that they lasted till Moskow and my younger daughter got the orange from Prague.

Was it sentimental of me to be so touched by this? I pictured my own small childhood bedroom on Christmas morning, and the grey knee-length sock of an eight-year-old lumpy with presents. At the bottom there was always an orange and a few walnuts. Even then it crossed one's mind that these were of small value. Weren't there plenty more downstairs in the Christmas bowls? But these were special, and were put aside on the bedroom table for later consumption. Is it nostalgia for a lost paradise, sharpened by middle age, that makes me think those childhood gifts had a proper proportion? Boris' daughter received an orange from Prague, a poignant and beautiful gift, because it was all he was able to bring. No, it is sentimental. I bet she would have preferred the puppet theatre and twelve fairy-tale Bohemian puppets I brought home for *my* daughter.

Shopping in Wenceslas Square

The day after Boris left, Caroline, Kate, and I became unashamed tourists, lunching in the stylish art nouveau Hotel Paris, and then going shopping. Half-way down Wenceslas Square was a shop with the unprepossessing name of *Hracky* – which simply means 'toyshop'. Inside there were many *hrackys*, none with individual names because at that time they were still state-owned. It was here that I bought the toy theatre.

The stage was a rectangular box made of pale green hardboard, about the size of a briefcase. It contained eight slots to take the wooden uprights which support the proscenium arch, backcloth, and wings. The cardboard scenery slides into grooves in the uprights.

There were four different stage sets which we subsequently named: 'Inside the woodman's cottage', 'Inside the royal palace', 'In a tangled moonlit forest', and 'The village beneath the fairy castle'. These traditional scenes captured the ambiguities of their subjects: the beautiful forest also portended magic and evil spirits; the alluring cottage kitchen might be where a lost child is fed by the honest gamekeeper, or eaten by Baba Jaga, the witchlike wicked granny. The sunlit castle taunts the downtrodden classes with the dream of the luxury to be found inside. Potential uprising is personified by the ragged boy growing aware of his youthful strength, but the heraldic grandeur of the kingly hall is heavy with the weaponry of subjugation.

These are the scenes of fairy tales, but also the backdrops of experience. And, although they are intended to depict a world of make-believe, the adult knows, what the child only senses as a tingle down the spine, that such fantasies, far from being a trivial diversion, penetrate the depths of the psyche: self-identity, eternal meaning, death, good and evil.

On to this stage the puppet master, be she young or be she old, is able to introduce twelve characters with whom she must tell her story.

Baba Jaga is dressed in black with black boots and a mottled headscarf tied round her head. Her hands and face are slime green. She has a monstrous nose, a massive misshapen conk; one eye is covered with a bright green cataract, the other half closed and furtive. Which does she see through? Is she all-seeing through the reptilian green eye, or does she peep furtively through the closed one, catching her victim off guard? She is the witch, the supernatural hag, the old woman who frightens children, and maybe even *eats* them.

There are two children, fresh and innocent. He has blond hair and a freckled nose, she bright blue eyes and a red hood. They are Hansel and Gretel, Jenicek and Marenka, John and Mary, Red Riding Hood, Jack of the beanstalk – universal children, uncorrupted and vulnerable, at risk in the world of adult predation.

The king and princess also symbolize goodness. Benign and priestly, with a fluffy white beard and a purple robe, he is a cross between good King Wenceslas and God. The princess is dressed as a bride adorned for her husband, in the white of a virgin, Snow White, a symbol of purity and the beauty of innocence.

Her counterpart is the devil, half-man, half-beast. He has the horns of a bull, one human foot, and one cloven hoof. His teeth, which sparkle in a grey-black face, could be vampires' fangs, and his green eyes with black pupils radiate lust, greed, and jealousy. He is the despoiler, the corrupter, the dark and evil side of personality.

Then there is Vodnik, the waterman. He too is green, but bright green like a frog, with popping red eyes and a big red smile. His hair is green and he wears an ill-fitting green tail-coat and red boots. Vodnik sits by the water on a willow trunk in the full moon, stitching his fishing pots. If you are naughty and play near the water, you will go to the waterman. He can drag children down under the water, and they will never be seen again. He keeps souls captive in his pots. But he can do miracles too. People go to the waterman with their problems and their illnesses. He is a witch doctor – ambiguously both bad and good.

Myslivec, the gamekeeper, embodies justice. He wears a dashing green hat with a feather in it, like Robin Hood. His high cheekbones, rugged features and trim grey beard give him an honest and reliable appearance, strong enough to be firm with offenders. He even wears a tie. From his cottage in the middle of the forest he looks after the forest and its inhabitants. But Myslivec is only human and not always a match for the supernatural forces of evil.

Kasparek, the 'little red one', is a miniature clown, a clever joker, a sort of 'Pinocchio'. He helps the poor who hear him coming because of the bells on his hat.

POSTCARDS ON THE WAY TO HEAVEN

Yet the last shall be first and the first shall be last. Daft Johnny, Honza Hloupy, is the cleverest of all. He does nothing and goes about with a vacant expression on his face. His arms are long and his hands dangle as if incapable of any co-ordinated act. He is the village idiot, a bit like the 'Good Soldier Schleg'. One day his mother cooks him a doughnut which he shares with the ants. When he arrives at a sad city, he visits the cottage of an old lady, and learns that there is a dragon in the region which has been eating young girls. He visits the castle and finds that the princes and young noblemen have all tried and failed to kill it. But, with the help of the ants and a magic sword, Honza Hloupy slays the dragon. The saviour is the one who is the least worldly, the least noble, the butt of other people's humour, the antithesis of human success.

I don't know how accurate my interpretation of these puppets is. I was told the stories by a Czech, whom I married to an English bride in 1991. Instead of marriage 'preparation', which some clergy make rather a meal of, we talked about Czech folklore, which was a relief to me, because, although I do a good line in the spiritual meaning of marriage, I would not presume to advise on mortgages, or the birds and the bees. But accuracy is not the point as far as the imagination is concerned. The children who used our puppet theatre enacted the stories of Cinderellla, Jack and the Beanstalk, Snow White, Red Riding Hood, Rumpelstiltskin, Sleeping Beauty. They were able to superimpose their own tradition and their own imaginations on these universal symbols of good and evil.

How am I to sum up the Prague pilgrimage? With an explanation? An allegorical interpretation like the appendix to the parable of the sower? When asked to explain a difficult étude, Schumann sat down and played it a second time. But I will not be mulish about this.

J. G. Davies says that a pilgrimage centre is 'a place of intersection between everyday life and the life of God.'[2] Prague, of course, was precisely *not* everyday life for me; it was so different that my experiences there were seen as if through a magnifying glass. I suppose the obvious interpretation of Davies' view is that you bring your everyday life to the holy place for renewal and expiation: your sickness to Lourdes or Loreto, your spiritual curiosity to Jerusalem, offering your ordinary self to God in the hope of transformation. This needn't, of course, involve international travel. Many people bring domestic worries, problems of relationship and romance, or prayers for a sick relative, to their local church, their local holy place. I wasn't particularly conscious of taking my own everyday life to Prague (although doubtless I did), but the heightened awareness that this unusual experience induced enabled me to see in the commonplaces of life that I met there signs of the holy – a Russian song, an orange, a set of children's puppets. These things mediated God more effectively than the hours spent meditating on the floor of the great tent. Sometimes we need to distance ourselves from our own everydayness in order to see the holiness that actually pervades it.

He who has ears to hear let him hear.
And she who has eyes to see let her see.

Cheers Boris!

CHAPTER 9

HEAVEN

When I go to heab'n gonna put on my shoes, gonna walk all ober God's heab'n.
Negro Spiritual

My master is of churlish disposition,
And little recks to find the way to heaven
By doing deeds of hospitality.
As You Like It (Act 2.IV)

When I was ten or eleven I remember going by coach to Clacton-on-Sea on the annual Sunday School outing. The outing was a relic of the old days when churches took their children out of East London to the seaside, for what would be for most of them the only day away from home during the whole of the summer. Ours was a high principled, puritanical church: all the adults were teetotallers, and many of the members refused to have milk or papers delivered on Sundays because they believed it was wrong to force others to break the observance of the Lord's Day.

On the way home from Clacton we always had a singsong, and I remember particularly, *Oh, you'll never get to heaven*. 'Oh, you'll never get to heaven in an old Ford car, 'cos an old Ford car won't get that far. Oh, you'll never get to heaven in a limousine, 'cos the Lord don't stock no gasoline. Oh, you'll never get to heaven in a comet jet, 'cos the Lord ain't got no runways yet.' Then there was the chorus, 'I ain't gonna grieve my Lord no more.' The song excited me because it seemed daring and subversive, sending up both heaven and God. What surprised me was that the grown-ups joined in with equal gusto, as if they too needed a bit of light relief from the seriousness of their church-going lives, summed up in the words, carved in stone, above the church door, 'This is the gate of heaven'.

So far I have been sending postcards from the road to Heaven; now I have the almost impossible task of speaking of heaven itself. Heaven is usually thought of as belonging to the future, either as a place you might be lucky enough to go to when you die, or as the community of those who are saved after the last judgement, when Christ, the Son of Man, comes on the clouds of heaven in power and great glory (Matthew 24.30). Sometimes it is conceived as an eternal city, a garden of perpetual spring and summer, a great feast, or meeting with God face to face. All these images combine in Bernard of Cluny's great hymn, *Jerusalem the golden*: the heavenly city, like the Promised Land, is 'with milk and honey blest', the sound of the city is 'the shout of them that feast', the 'daylight is serene', and the pastures have a 'glorious sheen'. The throne of David has become the throne of God, and the Prince of this ideal, and idealized, city-state is Christ himself.

Heaven right here on earth

But heaven also belongs to the present. Whether Jesus thought of the kingdom of God as belonging to the future, or something already established in his own ministry is an issue hotly debated by scholars. The probable answer is: a bit of both. At the Last Supper he says that he will not drink wine again until he drinks it in the kingdom of God (Mark 14.25), whereas, when he is accused of casting out demons in the name of Beelzebub, he says that if his healing comes from God, then 'the Kingdom of God has come upon you' (Matthew 12.28). This suggests that heaven can be both present and future, and that what is ultimately important for Christianity is not exclusively reserved until the end of time, but discernable here and now. That's what this book has been about – the sparklingly diverse images and experiences that are capable of revealing God.

It is sometimes said that a person can be too heavenly-minded to be of any earthly use; this could be extended to saying that if you want to find God, don't try looking *too* far away. Two stories illustrate this. One February when there were unusually severe floods, a Christian was stranded on the roof of his bungalow, and the waters were rising. First, a diver peered over the gutter and offered to help. 'No thanks,' said the Christian, 'God will save me.' The waters continued to rise. Then someone in a boat offered to row him to safety. 'No thanks,' said the Christian, 'God will save me'. By the time the Christian was standing on the ridge of his roof, a helicopter hovered overhead, a ladder was let down, and he was waved aboard. 'No thanks,' shouted the Christian, 'God will save me'. Eventually, he drowned. When he got to heaven he asked God why he had not saved him. God said, 'I sent a diver, a rowing-boat, and a helicopter. What more could I do?'

The second is a story, told by Tolstoy, of a cobbler who longs to meet Christ. In his prayers Christ tells him that he will meet him that very day. He looks out at the pavement from his workshop window, but Christ doesn't come. Then he sees a snow sweeper, fingers frozen to the bone, and invites him in to warm himself by the fire. Next he takes compassion on a mother and her starving child, and gives them something to eat. Later, he sees boys stealing apples from an old woman's basket, and goes out to help her. At the end of the day, when he closes the shop, Christ still hasn't come, and he is disconsolate. At his prayers that night he complains that God has failed to keep his promise to visit him, but Christ protests that he did come, and in the corner of the room appears a vision first of the snow sweeper, then the mother, and finally the old woman.

These are tales of the immanence of God, the here-and-nowness of the kingdom of heaven, the touchability of God.

(Remember Graham Greene's Spanish priest: 'I do not believe in God, I touch him'.) But the other side of the coin is just as important: the transcendence of God, the eternity of God, and therefore hope for the future.

Life in the World to Come

The Bible builds up a series of visionary images for heaven that look to the future and spring naturally out of the adversity experienced by the Jews, especially exile, and political insecurity. Thus the Jews dream of a homecoming to a politically secure Jerusalem, a paradise of broad rivers and streams, and the restoration of the kingdom as it was in the palmy days of King David. This is a theme taken up by the black slaves of America, whose spiritual songs look forward from the extreme hardship of bondage to the consolation of heaven – *Steal away to Jesus*, *Swing low, sweet chariot, coming for to carry me home*, and *Heab'n*.

The idea of a good time coming also features in the New Testament. Jesus' parable of the Rich Man and Lazarus (Luke 16.19–31) describes how in the afterlife the fortunes of the two men, one rich and one poor, are reversed.

The Book of Revelation develops the futuristic theme, and suggests a vast international crowd gathered outside God's palace, chanting 'Blessed be God for ever and ever' (Revelation 7.12). The scene is not unlike the newsreel pictures of the crowds gathered outside Buckingham Palace at the end of the Second World War, and the sentiment is not dissimilar either – we have just been through a great tribulation, and now we look forward to a time when there will be no hunger, or pain, or war, or sadness, or droughts, or natural disasters. In Revelation chapter 21 John sees the new Jerusalem descending from heaven, and God coming to earth to put an end to all history, death and suffering with the words, 'Behold, I make all things new'.

Then, of course, Jesus' key picture of heaven is that of a

banquet, or feast, or wedding reception. But I'm going to save the party for the end.

In the most popular of heavenly texts, Jesus says that in his Father's house there are many mansions (John 14.2). Translators have debated whether a mansion is a place where you remain permanently, or a place where you rest for a while before moving on. William Temple said that they were 'wayside caravanserais – shelters at stages along the road where travellers may rest on their journey.'[1] It was also the custom for travellers to send ahead an advance messenger, or interpreter, to make preparations for their arrival at the next resting-place. This makes special sense of Jesus' comment, 'If it were not so, would I have told you that I go to prepare a place for you'. It also extends the journeying image into heaven, as if the wilderness and nomadic roots of the Judaeo/Christian religion should not be forgotten even there – my ancestor was a wandering Aramaean, a homeless refugee!

However, modern English usage has rather gentrified the word 'mansion' into a sort of grand house with electrically controlled gates, whereas originally it denoted any dwelling however humble. So I would like to expand the mansion image in yet another direction by reference to a staging convention in the production of medieval mystery plays. The different scenes, such as the nativity, crucifixion, and resurrection, were staged in a series of *mansions*, or cubicles, constructed around the inside periphery of the church. These mansions were like mini-theatres, and sometimes curtains were used so that actors could be revealed at a particular moment, thus heightening the dramatic impact. When the mystery plays were taken out of the churches and on to the streets, the convention of using mansions was retained. A sixteenth-century illustration of the mansions used for the Valenciennes mystery plays shows constructions with steps rising to an elevated stage, and pillars supporting neo-classical canopies, incidentally creating a proscenium arch. These mansions are for disclosure, revelation, and enlightenment.

The peasants who watched couldn't read, and this was their Bible. In my Father's house there are many mansions, many disclosures, many dramatic surprises.

If that fragment of exegesis enlightens the text, it is of course only by quirk of the English translation, and nothing to do with the original Greek. But I have been arguing in this book that such expansions of the image repertoire are theologically valid and part of the continuing unravelling of the mystery of God.

Paradise Regained

Or there is the image of the heavenly garden, so often the idealized backdrop for the illuminations in medieval manuscripts, where all things harmonize; the grapes are being carried to the presses and the corn to the granary – raw materials for the eucharistic feast. The Bible's first word on paradise is the description of the Garden of Eden and the tree at its centre which mesmerized Eve with its promise of wisdom and sensual delight. Eden was heaven on earth until Eve took the apple and Adam ate. Then they knew good and evil, and were expelled from paradise. It is as if innocence must be suspended between promise and fulfilment, and the garden image of spring and harvest-in-progress symbolizes exactly that. My favourite postcard from Spain is of the Alhambra Gardens in Granada profuse with oranges and wisteria, in the spring sunshine, against the backdrop of the snow-clad Sierra Nevada. If I could add the babble of clear water in the watercourses, you would know you were in heaven.

Paradise lost becomes paradise regained in the Easter gardens of the gospels, in the transition from the Garden of Gethsemane to the garden of the resurrection. This is Eden reversed: 'as in Adam all die, so also in Christ shall all be made alive' (1 Corinthians 15.22). And the imagery expands: just as Adam and Eve heard the voice of the Lord God walking in the garden, so Mary Magdalene hears the voice of Christ and thinks he is the gardener. In the iconography of painting, Eve, who instigated the fall by taking the forbidden fruit, is replaced by the Blessed Virgin Mary, who instigated redemption by humbly accepting the motherhood of the Redeemer. In literature the cross is frequently referred to as the 'tree', and as the iconography of the cross develops in art, it begins to sprout foliage, as in Michelangelo's *Vatican Pietà* of 1499, symbolizing that it is a tree of *life*, and perhaps the exceedingly beautiful tree that stands in the centre of the garden.

More of the same?

But a word of caution. I couldn't resist buying Julian Barnes' *A History of the World in $10\frac{1}{2}$ Chapters* – such a brilliant title. It begins with Noah's Ark and ends with heaven. The chapter on heaven is very naughty, you might think even blasphemous, but subversion on this subject was legitimized for me on the bus home from Clacton. The author finds himself in heaven. The breakfasts are wonderful, his golf improves by leaps and bounds, he eats lots of sturgeon and chips, and Leicester City keep winning the FA Cup. But, perfection has its downside: what is the fun in getting round the golf course in 18 strokes? And wouldn't it be nice to feel tired afterwards, but there is no fatigue in heaven. So he has a word with his guardian angel. 'Oh yes,' she says, 'we often get people asking for bad weather, for instance, or for something to go wrong ... Some of them ask for pain.'[2]

What he exposes is the inherent weakness of pictures of heaven drawn from earthly experience, because they always seem to end up as a desire for more of the same, without the complications and disadvantages of this world. So I think we have to set aside the marble halls, and the thrones, and the flowering deserts, and concentrate on the more abstract notions of hope and relationship. We have to recognize the final inadequacy of imagery and realize that all that we are able to say is by way of introduction; 'for we know in part and we prophesy in part. But when that which is perfect is come, then that which is in part shall be done away ... for now we see through a glass, darkly; but then face to face' (1 Corinthians 13).

The Meaning of Life Supper

It is this seeing *face to face* that is the key, and that brings me Jesus' invitation to the grand party to end all parties. The New English Bible begins the famous parable with the words 'A man was giving a *big dinner-party*' (Luke 14.16). I am afraid I simply can't think of the messianic banquet as a dinner-party – it's such a very middle-class concept, much associated with the braying classes.

So what shall I call this meal in the parable, which crosses all social barriers? How about the Authorised Version's 'great supper'? This is no cosy supper for friends, but a *great* supper, not unlike, perhaps, those occasions in Thomas Hardy in the great hall or the barn where gentry and tenants together eat, drink, and make merry, with music and dancing. These are occasions, especially at Christmas and harvest, keenly anticipated, particularly by the poorer members of the community, for whom a feast at the landowner's expense is a seasonal highlight, much anticipated and affectionately looked back on.

In the parable, the wealthier members of the community have better things to do than to hob and nob. In modern terms, one has just bought a weekend cottage in the country and has some decorating to do; another has bought a classic Bentley and wants to drive out along the Cotswold lanes; another has just got married, and they are so absorbed in each other that they need all the 'quality time' they can get. What none of these three has realized is that they have been invited to the Great Meaning of Life Supper. Those who attend will discover what it is all about; those who have been diverted will find pleasure in their diversions, but they will miss out on the secret of the kingdom of God.

The parable of the Wise and Foolish Virgins (Matthew 25.1–13) makes a similar point: heaven is the wedding reception, and the guests must be ready and waiting when the bridegroom comes, or they won't get in to the meaning of life celebrations. Be ready for the judgement of God, because it will come unexpectedly.

Is it possible to tease out the meaning in the 'Meaning of Life Supper' from these stories, or are they simply about being prepared? At one level of course Jesus' repeated use of the image of the heavenly banquet is susceptible to the Julian Barnes' criticism – even sturgeon and chips, washed down with Chateau D'Yquem 1945, gets boring after a time. But banquets are about hospitality, friendship, and welcome; wedding banquets are about the celebration of love, both physical and spiritual; and as the poor are brought in from the highways and byways, so the barriers of social distinction are broken down creating a vision of justice that matches the apocalyptic hope of the Book of Revelation.

Luke gives a paradoxical spin to the wise and foolish virgins story. Jesus tells his disciples (Luke 12.37) to be like servants who wait up for the return of their master who has been a guest at the marriage feast. Then he will come in, make them sit at the table, and serve them. This is the 'first shall be last, and last shall be first' motif. George Herbert takes up this reference in his poem *Love*, which comes at the end of his cycle of poems under the general title, *The Church*.

> Love bade me welcome: yet my soul drew back,
>   Guiltie of dust and sinne.
> But quick-ey'd Love, observing me grow slack
>   From my first entrance in,
> Drew nearer to me, sweetly questioning,
>   If I lack'd any thing.

HEAVEN

> A guest, I answer'd, worthy to be here:
>   Love said, You shall be he.
> I the unkinde, ungratefull? Ah my deare,
>   I cannot look on thee.
> Love took my hand, and smiling did reply,
>   Who made the eyes but I?
>
> Truth Lord, but I have marr'd them: let my shame
>   Go where it doth deserve.
> And know you not, sayes Love, who bore the blame?
>   My deare, then I will serve.
> You must sit down, sayes Love, and taste my meat:
>   So I did sit and eat.

This is a poem about heaven, in which Christ shows such grace and attentive hospitality that the embarrassed guest is immediately put at ease and given the honour of a seat at Christ's table. I conclude from this that ultimate meaning has something to do with acceptance and relationship. It is not about pleasure in the consumerist sense of 'more of the same without the problems', but about the fulfilment which comes from self-giving and acceptance, both on the part of God and on the part of individual human beings.

In *As You Like It* Shakespeare recognizes that deeds of hospitality pave the way to heaven, and he develops the theme in Act 2 scene 7 where the banished Duke Senior and his merry men are about to sit down to their dinner in the wintry Forest of Arden, when suddenly the hero Orlando, also alienated from the court, breaks in violently demanding food. He thinks he must take it with menaces, but is amazed to be welcomed and asked to sit at the table. The Duke says,

> True it is that we have seen better days,
> And have with holy bell been knoll'd to church,
> And sat at good men's feasts, and wiped our eyes
> Of drops that sacred pity hath engend'red;
> And therefore sit you down in gentleness ...

Better days, fellowship, and compassion have provided the vision of the transforming nature of hospitality, and it is that which saves them from savagery in the cruel forest.

Moreover, we cannot miss the eucharistic significance of the banquet. The heavenly banquet is prefigured in the gospels by a range of eating analogies. There is the wedding reception in Cana of Galilee (John 2.1-11) where Jesus changes water into wine, symbolically replacing the water of Pharisaic Judaism with the good wine of Christianity, and doing so with such prodigality (six jars holding 20 or 30 gallons) that there is more than enough for everyone. Who can miss the allusion that this is the wine that flows from Jesus, the 'true vine', and is drunk at the eucharist? Or the Feeding of the Five Thousand (Matthew 14.21) where five thousand people were satisfied on five loaves and two fish, and still there were twelve baskets of scraps left over. This sharing and this fulfilment is what it will be like in heaven, and what it is like in the eucharist. Then there is the meal at Emmaus where the resurrected Christ is not recognized until he breaks bread – the bread of the eucharist. And the story of the Miraculous Draught of Fishes (John 21.4-14) where the resurrected Christ indicates to the disciples where to cast their net for a catch, but is not fully recognized by them until he takes the bread and fish and gives it to them at breakfast. This story is both eucharistic and directly allusive to the Feeding of the Five Thousand, where bread and fish are the eucharistic elements.

Why then is this imagery so recurrent in the gospels? Because it contains the mystery of the kingdom of heaven; the mystery of communion between people and with God, which must be explored and cannot fully be explained. It is an idea poeticized by Cranmer's prayer of Humble Access in the Anglican Book of Common Prayer, 'Grant us therefore, gracious Lord, so to eat the flesh of thy dear Son, Jesus Christ ... that we may evermore dwell in him, and he in us'. This perhaps is heaven, this mutual incorporation, this living in the universal hope, and underlying order, and supporting love of God. This is seeing face to face, recognizing the actual relationship between God and creation, in which God pervades the whole of creation as meaning and love, crossing the barriers of time and space. Meaning is not a gloss we have invented and imposed on life, it is embedded in the creation.

This is what theology refers to as 'eschatology': the contemplation of the last things, the end and purpose of history, what ultimately matters. It is important for Christianity that this isn't reduced to a compensatory world of pie in the sky when you die, because what ultimately matters is a question that permeates every aspect of God talk – past, present, and future. That, I suspect, is why so many of Jesus' teachings about the future stress the urgency of immediate decision-making, because you never know at what hour the judgement will come. Suddenly it is too late, and the doors are closed, or you are ejected for not being clothed in the wedding garment of righteousness (Matthew 22.11), and the vultures are hovering to consume what remains (Luke 17.37).

We all have our eschatological experiences: it may be at a time of loss and bereavement, or when faced with a serious illness, or at the birth of a child, as your awesome responsibility for this new life registers. At times like these we might find ourselves asking the question, what *really* matters in life? When you take away all the superficialities, what are you left with? It is this experience, I think, that still leaves many people uttering the word 'God', not as an empty plea for meaning, but as an affirmation that there is a future with meaning and purpose in a creation in which each person finally is accepted as significant and valued by the God of love.

The Last Word on Feasting

When I was a child, the days before Christmas were days when our meals were almost austere, eating up bits and pieces from the larder, and having a simple diet because we knew that Christmas Day and Boxing Day would be days of feasting and indulgence. On Christmas morning my mother used to spread a table with tangerines and chocolates, crystallized figs, nuts, toffees, dates, turkish delight, sugared almonds and marzipan fruits, and we were allowed to stuff ourselves on these as we wished. It seemed like heaven. Nowadays there are parties from the beginning of December, so that by the time Christmas arrives the edge of your appetite can be so blunted that Christmas dinner resembles the latter stages of a pie-eating competition.

There needs to be a balance between having an appetite for the feast and being satisfied by it. It is a paradox which applies to many experiences, not least to a holiday where the excitement of the journey can overshadow the experience of arrival. If only you could be on holiday *and* maintain the excitement of the journey. It is similar with spirituality: searching for God is an indispensable aspect of finding him; and you have not found God if you are not still searching. Much as you think it would be nice to have the final solution, or to be saved on a once and for all basis, and to be absolutely certain of your salvation, you begin to see that such ideas are a deception – you always need hunger to make the feast satisfying.

Presumably, those who are compelled to come in to the great supper from the highways and hedges do not necessarily hold orthodox beliefs, they are not necessarily familiar with any uniform teaching of 'the' Church; they are simply cold and hungry, surprised and grateful to be asked. Their presence transforms an ordinary occasion into the 'Meaning of life supper', precisely because they are there in all their hunger, naïveté, and probably embarrassment, searching and looking.

NOTES

2 THE CHRISTIAN IMAGE REPERTOIRE

1. J. H. Newman, *Essay on the Development of Christian Doctrine* (1845), p. 40.
2. Valentine Cunningham, *In the Reading Gaol, Postmodernity, Texts, and History* (Blackwell 1994), p. 401.
3. George Steiner, *After Babel* (OUP 1975).
4. I owe this to discussion with Professor Brown in a seminar.

3 WHEN THE PENNY DROPS

1. Ian Ramsey, *Religious Language* (SCM 1957).
2. Ramsey, *Religious Language*, p. 51.
3. Philip Larkin, *Required Writing* (Faber and Faber 1983).

4 THE LIMITS OF IMAGERY

1. Keith Ward, *A Vision to Pursue* (SCM 1991).

5 GOD IN MUSIC

1. George Steiner, *Real Presences* (Faber and Faber 1989), p. 217.
2. Steiner, *Real Presences*, p. 20.
3. Laurens van der Post, *The Lost World of the Kalahari* (Penguin 1962), p. 224f.
4. This is discussed by Paul Davies in *The Mind of God, Science and the Search for Ultimate Meaning* (Penguin 1992), p. 144f and p. 175f.
5. Roger Penrose, *The Emperor's New Mind: Concerning Computers, Minds and the Laws of Physics* (OUP 1989), p. 97.
6. Hans Küng, *Mozart: Traces of Transcendence* (SCM 1992), p. 19.
7. *Collected Poems 1945–1990* (Phoenix 1993), p. 104.

NOTES

6 MEETING GOD AT THE EDGE OF FAITH

1. Graham Greene, *A Sort of Life* (The Bodley Head 1971), p. 85.
2. Marie-Françoise Allain, translated from the French by Guido Waldman, *The Other Man: Conversations with Graham Greene* (The Bodley Head 1983), p. 19.
3. Allain, *The Other Man*, p. 156.
4. Allain, *The Other Man*, p. 170.
5. Allain, *The Other Man*, p. 173.
6. *The Guardian*, 15 May, 1996.

7 WALKING WITH GOD

1. Steiner, *Real Presences*, p. 232.
2. J. G. Davies, *Pilgrimage Yesterday and Today: Why? Where? How?* (SCM 1988), p. 127.
3. Bruce Chatwin, *The Song Lines* (Picador 1988), p. 216.
4. Chatwin, *The Song Lines*, p. 213.
5. Gerhard von Rad, *Genesis* (SCM 1972), p. 325.
6. Martin Luther – quoted by Davies in *Pilgrimage Yesterday*.

8 A PILGRIMAGE TO PRAGUE

1. John Navone, *Seeking God in Story* (Collegeville, Minnesota, The Liturgical Press 1990), p. 173.
2. Davies, *Pilgrimage Yesterday*, p. 1.

9 HEAVEN

1. William Temple, *Reading in St John's Gospel*, Vol. 2 (Macmillan), p. 226.
2. Julian Barnes, *History of the World in $10\frac{1}{2}$ Chapters* (Jonathan Cape 1989).